WHAT EVERY
PARENT
NEEDS TO
KNOW ABOUT
SELF-INJURY

TONJA H. KRAUTTER

PUBLISHED BY FASTPENCIL, INC.

I dedicate this book to the many patients I have worked with through the years who have suffered from self-injury. It has been both an honor and a privilege to have shared their journey through treatment and recovery. Their courage, strength, and commitment to overcoming this devastating illness is an inspiration to all persons who believe they will never get better. They are proof that with proper treatment, a good support system, and the willingness and motivation to change, recovery is not only possible, it is probable. Thank you for sharing your journey with me.

Acknowledgements

I am a Practicing Clinical Psychologist who finds great meaning in helping others. I feel honored and privileged to work in the mental health field. In addition, I am a mother who draws inspiration and joy from raising two precious children. Both my family and my career are priorities in my life. I feel blessed to have created a balance between them.

The identification and understanding of the development of self- injury can leave a family feeling frustrated, frightened, confused, and defeated. My greatest hope in writing this book is to provide knowledge about self-injury to all families who are currently raising pre-teen, teenage, and young adult children in our society today. We are witnessing first hand a dramatic cultural phenomenon among our youth circled around the development of unhealthy coping mechanims. By acknowledging this shift, we are able to gain a better understanding of the complexities involved and offer the opportunity to help our children in both positive and healthy ways.

I would like to acknowledge the contributions of several people, without whom, I would not have completed this book.

To my incredible editor, Stacey Paris McCutcheon. Thank you for your interest and commitment to this book project. You inspired me to finish this book and start some new ones. You are wonderful!

To my dedicated readers, Dr. Fawn Powers and Karen Conterio. Thank you for your time and effort in reviewing this book. It is an honor and privilege to have your support and guidance.

To my good friend, Steve O'Deegan, for his hard work and commitment to the finalized product.

To the many people who supported me in my efforts and convinced me that this book was a must read for parents who are raising pre-teens and teenagers in society today: Andrea Ancha, Anthony Atwell, Rebecca Powers, Gale Uhl, Melissa Sorci, Veronica Saleh, Ann Martini, Betsy Cregger, Grace Shih, Judith Siegel, Christina Halsey, Tom Miller, Dennis Champion, Anne Takahashi, James Cosse (R.I.P.), Carole and Terry Brennan, Maritza and Frank Jensen, Sara Gray, Sara Pearson, Juana and Marty Olsen, and Janice O'Deegan.

To my amazing parents, Heidi and Al Krautter who instilled in me a strong work ethic. You always supported me and taught me to give back to the community. This book is a way for me to do that. To my brother, Torsten Krautter, and his wife, Kim, your love and support means a lot to me.

ACKNOWLEDGEMENTS

To my incredible husband, Jason, whose constant encouragement and reassurance during the development of this book was invaluable. To my two amazing sons, Tyler and Brody, who had to give up several hours of "mommy time" in order to allow for the completion of this book.

To my incredible patients who have been consistently open and honest with me about their experiences with self-injury. You are the source of my inspiration for writing this book. The readers ultimately have you to thank for their acquired information and knowledge.

Thank you for sharing your journey of treatment and recovery with me and with them.

Thank you all!!

CONTENTS

INTRODUCTION

As often as ten times a week, I receive calls from parents devastated to learn that their child is engaging in self-injurious behavior. Regardless of what it has been called (the bright red scream, the new-age anorexia, or the newest addiction) the practice of self-injury is on the rise. Shock, fear, anger, and confusion overwhelm parents when they are told that the child they have struggled to protect since birth is now choosing to harm herself. I use the feminine pronoun because while this phenomenon is not limited to one gender, it is more visible among females than males. It is also not limited to a particular age, race, culture or socioeconomic status.

It seems incomprehensible, especially to parents, that a child would take a knife, razor blade, lighter or fist and intentionally harm herself. Parents ask, "What is my child trying to achieve?" The answer, unfortunately, is not simple. There are multiple reasons why kids self-injure. Accordingly, helping them to recover from this problem must start with a thorough examination of the problem itself.

There is no denying that society evolves on a continual basis throughout time. I think most people would agree that this is not necessarily a bad thing. In fact, many changes are viewed as positive. However, this is not the case for all societal shifts. It is for this reason that I have created a book series entitled *What Every Parent Needs to Know About ...* that addresses a variety of topics. The sole purpose of this series is to inform and educate parents about dangerous trends and behaviors that are becoming increasingly common among youth in our country. Some of these trends have evolved gradually over the several decades; others are startling new phenomena. In either case, they are present in our society and therefore, our children must face many of them today.

This book, *What Every Parent Needs to Know About Self-Injury,* will discuss the emotional and physical challenges faced by individuals who strive to recover from self-injurious behavior. It will provide insight and understanding to parents who want to learn more about self-destructive behavior. By blending clinical expertise with personal stories, the book will offer guidance and demonstrate practical strategies that can be utilized by caregivers to help children who are currently suffering from this problem.

What Every Parent Needs to Know About Self-Injury will educate parents on all facets of the problem of self-injury including cause and effect, cultural forces, risk assessment, treatment planning, therapeutic fit, relapse, and relapse prevention. In addition, I hope that every parent will gain a thorough understanding of both the physical and psychological consequences of self-injury, and how this behavior may affect the child socially, educationally, and/or occupationally.

By exploring the roller-coaster of emotions that coincide with this condition, and providing strategies to help combat the problem, parents will gain a better understanding of which responses are helpful, and which are more likely to be detrimental in dealing with a child struggling with self-injury. Armed with these insights, parents will be better equipped to help their children through recovery. Ultimately, with proper understanding, support, and treatment, individuals can overcome self-injurious behavior.

****

I was inspired to write this book for three primary reasons. First, self-injury is still a largely misunderstood condition that affects millions of individuals in our country. I feel compelled to emphasize the fact that self-injury does not only affect the individual sufferer but the family as a whole. As you will see through the many illustrations presented in this book, parents and siblings struggle significantly when their loved ones face this problem. It is for this reason that I strongly encourage family involvement in the treatment and recovery process. Often family members are the greatest resource for the individual who is suffering since they are also living with it on a daily basis in their home.

The second source of inspiration for this book came from something I learned in my profession: Highly-stressed individuals need a means to relieve their internal tension. This certainly applies to individuals who self-harm. Some individuals deal with distress in positive, healthy ways such as exercise, journaling, and/or artistic outlets. Others turn to negative and unhealthy means of stress relief, including substance abuse, disordered eating and/or self-injury. For an individual who self-injures, it is usually a combination of this personal distress with certain personality traits, family dynamics and cultural influences, that leads to the onset and maintenance of this problem.

Once fully established, the problem can be viewed as a cycle of negativity that has destructive consequences for the individual, and in turn, for everyone else in the family unit. Mental health professionals constantly search for creative ways to reduce a patient's isolation and help them to obtain the support necessary to feel more under-stood. The opportunity to hear and learn from the stories of other individuals who have dealt with self-injurious behavior helps both patients and their families gain insight and feel less alone.

The third, and most important reason for writing this book, is to offer some tangible explanations and relief to parents confronted with a child who self-injures. Parents typically feel hopeless and helpless when their child has been identified with this condition. Perhaps this is mostly due to the fact that most kids who are diagnosed do not want to get help – at least not initially. This leaves the parents feeling like they are fighting to keep their child safe without their child's cooperation. This can be infuriating for parents who simply do not understand why they are hurting themselves.

In this book, I offer a psychological perspective on self-injury and discuss how parents can cope with their child's condition. I also discuss the consequences of self-injurious behavior in the home, and review ways in which family members can help. In addition, I share many personal stories from individuals who went through treatment and recovery. I know that there are thousands of people who have traveled the same path as families I reference in this book, and there will be thousands more to come. I hope that learning about the journeys of others through the complicated world of self-injury might somehow provide hope and solace to them.

In closing, I want to acknowledge that every child and family situation is different. I would never suggest that this book addresses all the issues and manifestations of a child who self-injures. As readers will discover, self-injury does frequently break the spirit of many individuals and their families for a period during treatment and recovery. For a while, many of the individuals presented in this book lost nearly all of the daily battles that recovery presented. On the other hand, they did manage to win the long-term battle through perseverance, family support, and the timely discovery of substantive information along the way. It is my sincere hope that *What Every Parent Needs to Know About Self-Injury* will increase the knowledge base of this condition while emboldening parents to believe that they, too, can survive their child's journey of recovery.

1

WHAT IS SELF-INJURY?

"When I cut, I want to draw blood. When I break, I want something to shatter. I want a trail that marks my pain."
- Amber, age 18

Self-injury, also known as self-mutilation, self-harm, or cutting, is a largely misunderstood condition that affects millions of people. It is a growing epidemic in our society and one that cannot simply be written off as teenage angst. Both teenagers and adults suffer from self-injurious behavior, and the number is on the rise. With a reported two million cases in the United States alone, this disorder has become rampant.

A PHYSICAL EXPRESSION OF EMOTIONAL PAIN
The formal definition of self-injury was created by Karen Conterio and Wendy Lader, authors of *Bodily*

Harm: The Breakthrough Healing Program for Self-Injurers (Hyperion, 1986). They write, "It is the deliberate mutilation of the body or a body part, not with the intent to commit suicide but as a way of managing emotions that seem too painful for words to express." The following quote from a patient in their book captures this sentiment succinctly: "How will you know I am hurting, if you cannot see my pain? To wear it on my skin, tells what words cannot explain." - C. Blount

Other patients concur with the idea that self-injury is a way to express physically what they cannot express verbally. Some patients cannot express their sadness while others cannot express their anger. Rebecca, who began cutting herself six months ago, concretely explains the reasons behind this behavior. She says, "Cutting became my cry for help when words could not do it for me. I wanted people to see how ugly I was, and how ugly I felt. I was tired of trying to explain how much I hurt on the inside. I wanted it to show it on the outside." Rebecca is experiencing great sadness. She is looking for a way to prove to others and to herself that her pain is real. She has difficulty expressing her pain (sadness) verbally, so she chooses to express it physically.

Stephanie illustrates this point as well. However, Stephanie is experiencing tremendous anger. She just turned eighteen and states, "I cannot believe I am now *officially* an adult. Not much has changed. Certainly not the way I feel about myself. Hate is a powerful feeling. It rises within me, there is no ceiling. I mark myself to show my pain. I do not yell and I never scream. I hold it all in and let it consume me. Then the pain comes. It flows through me - slow, smooth, gradual - always consuming. This feeling is much more tolerable than hate."

There are many reasons individuals self-injure, which we will discuss at great length later in this book. The two examples above give a small glimpse of how different emotions can lead to the addictive process of self-injury. Individuals use self-injurious behavior as a way to cope with their distressing emotions. The one common denominator is typically the individual's difficulty with verbal self-expression. Without this ability, the person is left with a physical means of communication.

WHO SELF-INJURES?

Although study estimates vary, it is generally believed that 13% to 25% of adolescents and young adults surveyed in schools have some history of self-injury. (Rodham & Hawton, 2009). While many of these individuals self-injure only once or twice and then stop, others begin to practice the behavior regularly. Studies of college populations have determined that roughly 6% of college students actively and habitually practice self-injury. While it is likely that this same 6% applies to adolescents as a group, middle schools are likely to have a higher percentage of students practicing self-injury, as the behavior most often begins between the ages of 14 and 16. (Whitlock, Eckenrode, et al., 2006; Gollust, Eisenberg, & Golberstein, 2008). However, individuals also begin injuring in childhood and as adults.

People of all age, gender, sexual orientation, and race self-harm. While self-injury is prevalent in both males and females, it is typically more visible among females. (Whitlock, Muehlenkamp, et al., 2009). Additionally, young people identifying as bisexual, or questioning are considered at higher risk than their heterosexual or homosexual peers. (Whitlock, Eckenrode, et al., 2006; Whitlock, Muehlenkamp, et al., 2009). Individuals from a wide variety of geographic, socioeconomic, and cultural backgrounds participate in this deliberate, repetitive, and destructive behavior.

The reasons behind the need to self-injure are complex and often neglected or misunderstood. As a result, the behavior is frequently kept secret, which suggests that the number of reported cases is significantly lower than the number of actual cases in our country. Most individuals do not willingly seek treatment. If they do enter treatment, it is usually because a loved one insists on intervention. The person most likely to enter treatment is from a middle-to-upper-class family, with average-to-high intelligence and low self-esteem.

Nadia fits this description perfectly. She is 17 years old, bright, and from an upper-class family. She did not want to get help for self-harm. Nadia's parents "forced her into treatment." She kept it a secret for several years before they discovered cuts on her arm. Nadia was extremely angry when she entered therapy. She believed that her parents were making "a big deal out of nothing," and had no desire to share her thoughts and feelings with a complete stranger. She acknowledged that she rarely shared her thoughts and feelings even with people she was close to in her life.

However, through the course of treatment, Nadia began to open up. She admitted that she often felt empty inside. In a therapeutic journal assignment, she wrote, "Sometimes I perceive my world in shades of grey, like a black and white TV show. When I don't see color, when I *feel grey*, I feel no emotion other than sadness. Yet I don't feel sad enough to cry. It is a superficial sadness that tenaciously covers my other emotions so that I can't reach them. When *feeling grey*, I'm numb to the world around me and I am numb to myself. This is what entices me to cut. I want to see red. I want to see color. I want to *feel* something."

It is not uncommon for individuals who self-injure to experience this kind of emptiness, and to use self-harm as a way to experience some sort of feeling. Physical pain helps them to feel alive and not devoid of emotion. Human beings have the ability to feel things deeply. For many individuals who self-harm, seeing blood helps them to feel human.

Many individuals who self-injure report some form of abuse (physical, emotional, or sexual) during their childhood. Van der Kolk, Perry, and Herman (1991) conducted a study of individuals who exhibited cutting behavior. They found that exposure to physical abuse or sexual abuse, physical or emotional neglect, and chaotic family conditions during childhood, latency, and adolescence, were reliable predictors of the amount and the severity of cutting.

Sexual abuse victims were most likely of all to cut. The resulting trauma experienced by the individual can be an underlying cause of self-injurious behavior. This is true for Cathy. She was fifteen and a sophomore in high school when she was brutally raped while on vacation with her family in the Caribbean. Cathy is twenty-two now, and remembers that day as if it were yesterday. Following is one of the poems she wrote to try to make sense of what she was feeling:

> *Another day, another cut;*
> *pain, release, this island of sanity.*
> *Unreal, decaying, it's anything but;*
> *weeping, hating, testing morality.*
> *Blood, flowing like a stream; rolling down my arm;*
> *Drifting in a dream; finally feeling so calm.*
> *It's just another scar; no harm done so far;*
> *Maybe, when I'm pissed; I'll finally slash my wrists.*
> *Scars upon my body, more upon my heart;*
> *No one in my life; destined to live apart.*
> *My heart aches so bad; it's literally driving me mad.*
> *Things would be just fine, if only I could see the divine,*
> *I dream the past is gone and a new day will dawn.*

TYPES OF SELF-INJURY

The most common form of self-injury is cutting. There are many objects that individuals use to cut themselves with, including knives, razor blades, and glass. However, individuals who self-injure are not limited to these items. In fact many use instruments that most people would not even think of as something that could cause bodily harm. For example, it is not uncommon for self-injurers to use push pins, paper clips, nail files or staples to inflict injury.

It is also not uncommon for self-injurers to transform a harmless object into a sharp instrument to be used for self-harm. For example, Haley was hospitalized for suicidal ideation last spring. She was known on the hospital ward as a "cutter." She was placed on suicide watch and almost everything that could cause harm was removed from her room. She was only allowed a marker and paper for journaling. Each day she sharpened the marker's cap with her teeth, creating a pointed edge she used to cut her arms and legs when she felt the desire. She also gave herself paper cuts with the edges of the paper that was provided to her on a daily basis.

Hillary was Haley's roommate. She took the hooks that held the curtains in place and used them to scratch her arms and legs before going to bed at night. In addition, she found sharp pieces of metal protruding from one of the legs under a table in the TV room and while still attached, used them to scratch her feet and ankles.

Clearly, if someone is motivated to self-injure they will find a way. The solution is not to try to take away every item that could be used for self-harm, since that would be next to impossible. Instead, the goal is to help the individual control the desire to self-harm, and to help them better tolerate the overwhelming feelings that are present in their lives (See Chapter 8).

The second most common form of self-injury is burning. Like cutting, there are a variety of implements an individual may use in order to burn herself, including a lighter, matches, cigarette, cigar, candle, stove top, and/or a piece of metal that has been heated by fire. Joey, 17 years old, has been burning different parts of his body since he was 11. He remembers the first time he burned himself in a game of chicken with his friend. He and his friend put a burning cigarette between their arms and the first person to pull away was bequeathed with the title of "chicken."

Joey was determined to win the game. He recalls, "Winning made me feel tough. I was able to tolerate the physical pain longer than anyone else in my grade." Joey developed a belief system in which tolerating physical pain made him strong and respected by his peers. He received positive reinforcement for being "the toughest kid at school." Joey took great pleasure in challenging everyone he knew to the game of chicken.

When the game lost its novelty and others lost interest in playing, Joey began to play the game with himself. This time, he competed against the clock. How long could he stand the pain? The longer the amount of time that passed, the stronger and more powerful he felt. It did not take him long to realize that every time he was feeling powerless, he could burn himself and regain a sense of strength and self-confidence.

ESCALATION

Although cutting and burning are the most commonly reported types of self-injurious behavior, there are others. For example, the person may scratch, hit, bite, kick, head bang, and/or pull out hair. These secondary types of self-injurious behavior are often considered *gateway behaviors* to other, more severe forms of harm. In other words, someone may begin self-injuring using one of the methods listed above, and then move to a more severe form of self-injurious behavior. In the most extreme cases, an individual might break their bones, amputate a limb or inject toxins into their body. Although these behaviors are not common, they do occur.

There are various reasons why an individual might transition to a more severe form of self-injurious behavior. The two most cited reasons are: (1) to achieve greater mastery over distressful feelings, and (2) because superficial wounds do not provide the same "high" as do more severe wounds. In both cases, the individual increases the severity of bodily harm to achieve a specific goal.

Amber remembers making this transition. She clearly recalls her first time inflicting bodily harm. She writes, "Self-injury controlled my life for the better part of eight or nine months and what started it all I will never forget. I had a bad day at field hockey practice and I had finally had enough. Between pressures from school, my mom, field hockey and trying to deal with my own inner turmoil, I finally snapped. I came home so angry and so hurt; I didn't know how to let it out. I could feel the tension growing inside me, just getting worse and worse and so I did the only thing that made sense to me. I began to hit myself with my hockey stick. I mostly stuck to my feet and ankles, but I hit my hands some too.

It didn't make me feel better though. I needed more. So I went to the kitchen, got the sharpest knife I could find, and slowly ran it over my ankles. It was weird because I actually started to feel better. All that tension that was rising inside of me was released and seemed to flow out of me along with the blood. Hurting myself, at the time, was the only thing that made me feel better. From that time on, whenever something bad happened, I'd run right for the closest knife and start cutting."

ACCESSIBILITY

It is important to realize if a person engages in self-injury, it is likely that they will keep their instrument of choice accessible at all times. It may be hidden somewhere on their body, such as in a pocket, sock or shoe; or in a safe place nearby such as in their car, purse or wallet. Many self-injurers find it soothing to have the implement close by. Knowing they have a coping mechanism, or an instant "quick fix" for overwhelming emotions, is comforting and makes them feel at ease.

Joey recalls keeping a lighter with him at all times. He kept several in his car for easy access, he had one in every jacket pocket, and he hid one in his shoe when he knew the others would not be available. Sara knew her mother was aware of her self-injurious behavior and that she was terribly worried about her. Accordingly, Sara always tried to hide the behavior as well as the devices that she used to self-harm. Her instrument of choice was a razor blade. She recalls hiding them everywhere; in her purse, in her folders at school, under her foot in her shoe, and even in her hair when it was pulled up in a bun.

Elaine, a 35-year-old business executive, chose glass. She carried a piece of glass in her purse so that it was always with her. That way she could even slip out of an important business meeting and excuse herself to use the restroom, purse in hand, if tensions climbed too high.

Amber had designated places where she could go to cut, and carried a knife around with her wherever she went. She had one by her bed, and one in her desk, and if she went somewhere for the weekend, a knife came with her there too.

How is Self-Injury Discovered?

Self-injury is not a new phenomenon. Documentation of this behavior dates back to biblical times. The reason for the tremendous increase in publicity around this behavior in the past few years is directly connected to the increased number of cases reported in a variety of settings. Elementary, middle, and high school campuses are all identifying individuals who are engaging in this behavior much more frequently than in the past. Teachers are often the first to discover the problem and are often the ones who inform the child's parent. This is how Sierra's parents found out.

Sierra had just entered high school. The change from middle school to high school was not easy for her. Her mother described her as "a girl who strives for perfection in everything she does." She noted that even as a little girl, she put a lot of pressure on herself. Unfortunately, her high expectations often led to disappointment.

Sierra agreed that if she is less than perfect in her eyes or in the eyes of others, she becomes overwhelmingly distraught. As a way to cope with this distress, she began beating herself up both figuratively and literally. She started scratching her arms and legs in the beginning of her freshman year. By mid-year, she added a routine of punching herself in the stomach every time she got less than a 95% on a test. Although this helped her relieve her frustration to some degree, the scratching and punching did not give her the release she was looking for. She began cutting herself, using an X-Acto knife. She found it ironic that it was the same knife she used to perfect her art projects at home.

One day, at the end of her freshman year, she was out at PE. She always wore long sleeves to hide her cuts. After a grueling hour of field hockey, she returned to English class unaware that blood was seeping through her sleeve. Her English teacher noticed it right away when she raised her hand in class to answer a question. She was sent to the nurse who, in turn, sent her to the emergency room for stitches. The intense game of field hockey had re-opened a wound. Getting hit in the arm with the stick did not help either.

Upon entering treatment, Sierra tried to describe what led to her self-injurious behavior. She wrote in a journal entry, "At fifteen, before I have even finished my freshman year in high school, I already have a concept of what seems like immense pressure and stress. This is a feeling sewn deeply into me, a memory I can never erase. This pressure, coming from within, leads directly to my desire to self-harm. Although I cannot escape the memory, I can erase the tension and pressure that consume me in a given moment on a given day. Being the perfectionist that I am, I have always doubted myself, what I am capable of, and whether I am good enough. With help I am learning to break free of this habit, but the desire for perfection may always linger in the back of my mind."

In addition to middle schools and high schools, universities, jails, and work settings are seeing their fair share of self-injurious behavior. Elaine, mentioned previously, writes, "I have been with the same company since I graduated from college and have worked my way up to vice president. I am proud of my accomplishments. It is not easy for a woman to make it in a man's world, especially so early in life. I am a hard worker and I have good values. So why would I ever self-injure? The few close friends that know of my behavior ask me that question all of the time. They don't get it. Almost nobody ever does. For me, it is not about hating myself or punishing myself or feeling pain. It is a way to express what I am feeling and relieve the tension that goes along with my very stressful job. I am worried about being in a relationship and starting a family. I certainly do not want to model this destructive behavior for my children. I just know that when I self-injure, I feel better. It is an immediate relief from the distressing feelings that I have on a regular basis."

John is 22 years old. He spent one year in juvenile hall
where he knew several kids who utilized self-injury as a
coping mechanism. He never engaged in the behavior
himself until he went to jail at age 19 for involuntary man-
slaughter. John is an alcoholic. He has been in and out of
rehabilitation centers since he was 16. One evening, he
got extremely intoxicated and blacked out. He doesn't
remember getting into his car, driving 55 mph in a residential neighborhood, and crashing into the side of a
house. John killed a child who was asleep inside her bedroom. The first night he spent in jail, he began self-
injuring as way to punish himself. He commented, "I
could not hurt myself enough for what I did to that poor
kid and her family." The guards at the jail had to put John
on a round-the-clock safety watch as a precaution to keep
him safe.

Given the increasing number of self-injury cases, it is
no surprise that medical and psychiatric professionals are
inundated with patients seeking treatment for their
wounds, scars, and psychological distress. Hospitals and
doctors are often the first to identify self-injurious
behavior.   New and old scars are often observed
when patients come to emergency rooms for treatment, or
to their doctors' offices for check-ups. In the past, these
individuals were questioned about their injuries in
attempt to determine whether they were being abused by
another person.   However, in recent years, questions
regarding self-abuse have become much more prominent.

Brian is 17 years old and a junior in high school. His
parent found out about his self-injurious behavior when

he was taken to the emergency room for an unrelated incident. He broke his collar bone while playing in a football game at school. Brian explains, "I have always been described as 'the popular jock that gets good grades and all the girls.' Why would someone like me ever feel any pain, right? Wrong. I feel just as much pain and pressure as anyone else. It might sound weird hearing this from a guy, but society places too much pressure on teens to be a certain way and it's not only the girls who feel it. Society says that in order for girls to be popular and successful in life, they must be thin and beautiful. In order for guys to be popular and successful, they must be intelligent, good looking, and strong. If a teen falls short on any of these traits, he or she is ostracized and isolated. It's hard for me to meet all of the expectations that have been set by others. It is even harder for me to meet the ones I set for myself. When the tension becomes too much, I look for a way out. Self-mutilation provides me with that way."

WHY DOES SELF-INJURY FEEL ADDICTIVE

Self-injury is a coping mechanism that can feel addictive to the person who is doing it. When the individual self-injures, they experience a "rush" or "natural high." This feeling stems from a physiological process; beta endorphins are being released into the brain. After the initial "rush," the person finds herself in a peaceful and calm state of mind. This process is similar for individuals who exercise and experience the natural high that follows a good workout. These two feelings, the rush or natural high, followed by the state of calm, are what lead the person to engage in the behavior again and again. However, while the self-injurious behavior may *feel* very much out of the individual's control, it is clearly something the person *can* control with proper treatment and intervention.

Self-injury is a behavior that is chosen to deal with intense distress. The individual feels that finding a solution, or at least a substitute behavior that does not include self-harm, is futile; a belief that is reinforced every time unpredictable, overwhelming feelings in daily life result in the decision to self-injure again. Elaine, for example, has struggled with self-injury for over a decade. She states, "Almost immediately, I was hooked. It was a hard habit to break because I liked the way it made me feel – completely at peace with myself. Any time I was sad, upset or angry, which was most of the time back then, I would cut to feel better." Elaine cut herself every day, several times per day until she finally received treatment last year. She is now in recovery. She has not harmed herself in the past six months.

Many people who are recovered from self-injury still admit to feeling a desire to self-harm. It is not uncommon for these compulsions to be present for a long period of time following the last act of bodily harm. However, most individuals agree that, with time and intervention, the desires that they initially felt so strongly decrease in severity, duration, and frequency. Elaine, for example, reports that she had strong urges to self-injure for weeks after her last incident. She states, "At first it was all I could think about, but as time went on and I was able to tolerate my feelings better, my desire to cut decreased significantly. Now I rarely think about it at all."

FEELINGS AND COGNITIONS ASSOCIATED WITH SELF-INJURY

Individuals who self-injure often experience feelings of worthlessness or "inner badness." They frequently feel sad and "empty" inside. They may ruminate about death and dying, and ponder the usefulness of their lives. Nadia felt this way and relates, "I felt so empty inside that I often wondered if life was worth living. Self-injury helped me feel much more alive. It helped me feel something."

The self-injurer is often very fragile even if she presents as someone who is self-confident and strong. Amber, age 16, explains, "I have been battling depression for almost two years now, but you would never know by just looking at me." Most people see Amber as self-confident, beautiful, intelligent, and athletic. This led to her feeling misunderstood, invalidated, and unheard in many circumstances; all perceptions commonly cited by individuals who self-harm.

The way in which a self-injurer thinks and the way she feels seem to go hand in hand. Self-injurers characteristically have a particular thinking style. Their cognitions are focused on extremes, which is often referred to as "all or nothing" thinking. This dichotomous thinking style places the self-injurer at high risk for low self-esteem. Since there is no grey area within the dichotomy, the individual sees herself as either all good or all bad. With little room for partial gratification, it also sets the individual up for continual disappointment, particularly in relationships with others.

The self-injurer's self-esteem is highly dependent on external forces. Family, culture, and peer groups are all very influential in the lives of self-injurers, making them vulnerable when around these subsystems, particularly if they are feeling misunderstood. Joey comments, "I often blamed myself for events that were outside of my control and rarely took responsibility for my own actions and their consequences." Joeys' motivation to be successful came from the need to please others, not from within. He felt frequently hurt and disappointed in himself and those around him. Upon experiencing disappointment, he self-harmed to manage his feelings of "inner badness."

Lastly, the individual who self-injures often experiences great confusion, guilt, and shame for her actions. Nadia began cutting when she was 11 years old. She remembers the first day the problem began. She came home from school and heard her parents fighting. Their arguments had escalated in the past several months to an intensity that was overwhelming for her. As she stood in the laundry room listening to the anger and hostility that emanated from the room next door, she broke down and cried. However, her tears did not relieve the tension building inside of her.

As her tension increased so did her desire to do something about it. She desperately wanted to find a way "to make it go away." Without thinking, she frantically grabbed for a pair of sewing scissors that was on top of the washing machine and jabbed the pointed edge into her thigh. She immediately felt the pain, which began to pulsate through her leg. She watched the blood flow slowly "like a peaceful stream" down her thigh, across her ankle and onto the floor. Nadia stared at the blood and focused on her physical pain as a way to avoid her emotional distress. She was pleased that she no longer felt helpless in her situation and marveled in her newfound sense of control. It was at that very moment she knew she would self-injure again despite the fact that she knew what she was doing was wrong. The good feelings self-injury gave her outweighed the guilt and shame she experienced during and after the act of self-harm.

2

UNDERSTANDING SELF-INJURY

"I have been battling with self-injury for three years now, but you would never know it by just looking at me. I have been better, and I have definitely been worse, but one thing that is always the same is my scars. They are daily reminders of the places I have been and where I hope to never go again. But they are also an open door for people to see and to try to understand."

- Rebecca, age 16

Self-injury is a complex phenomenon that frightens and confuses most parents. It seems incomprehensible that a child would take a knife, razor blade, lighter or fist and intentionally harm herself. Parents do not understand what their child is trying to achieve. They only know that their child is engaging in a behavior that is self-destructive. It is painful for parents to watch, especially because they feel helpless to stop the behavior.

There are a variety of different factors and reasons that lead to the onset and maintenance of this problem. Accordingly, helping a child recover from this problem must start with a thorough examination of the problem itself. It is my hope that this chapter will help parents gain the understanding, knowledge, and insight necessary to support their child through treatment and recovery.

SELF-INJURY VS. SUICIDE

Self-injury is a coping mechanism. In contrast to what most people think, it is *not* a suicide attempt. In fact, the majority of self-injurers report that they engage in this behavior in an attempt to avoid suicidal ideation or action. The goal of self-injurious behavior is generally to feel better, not to end life. However, that does not mean that self-injury cannot unintentionally lead to death. If the person's behavior falls into a high-risk category (see below), it is possible that she may die unintentionally from self-harm.

For example, years ago I supervised interns who worked on a crisis hotline. One anonymous caller phoned in to talk about her severe depression. The caller denied any suicidal thoughts or intent. However, she did admit to a history of self-injurious behavior. At my request, the intern asked the caller if she was currently engaging in self-harm. The caller admitted that she was, and indicated that the cuts she was currently making on her inner thigh were bleeding heavily. Under direction from the intern, the caller was able to tell someone in her home about the injuries and was immediately rushed to the hospital. She received 78 stitches in her leg. The doctor reported that, although she may not have been trying to kill herself, she almost did.

Another factor to consider when evaluating self-injurious behavior versus suicidal intent is that both may be present at the same time. In other words, it is possible that the person engaging in self-injury is also actively suicidal. If this is the case, then their self-injurious behavior may in fact become a suicide attempt(s). Since some self-injurers are suicidal and some are not, it is very important to ask the person who is harming herself if she is having any thoughts about death and dying. If she is, further questioning is imperative. It is important to find out if she is actively thinking about killing herself and, if so, whether she has a plan in place to die.

If your child reports suicidal ideation especially with a plan in place, she must be taken immediately to the nearest emergency room for a more thorough safety assessment. Some parents are uncomfortable asking their children questions around suicide. The biggest fear is often that if they bring up the subject, their child who was not feeling suicidal will suddenly begin to think about killing herself. This is almost never the case. Think about yourself. If you are mentally stable and happy in your life and a friend comes up to you and asks if you are suicidal, would you all of a sudden start thinking about killing your-

self? I always tell parents not to be afraid to ask the tough
questions. If, to your knowledge, your child was not suicidal before and your questions reveal suicidal ideation,
you may have just saved her life.

If you do not want to ask your child these types of questions for whatever reason, do not worry. There are several types of mental health professionals who will cover
this topic as part of a thorough assessment. If you are worried about your child's safety, you can bring her to a therapist for this type of assessment. If she is unwilling to talk
to a therapist in an office, you can contact an adolescent crisis mobile unit (most counties have them). These
mobile units are staffed by trained mental health professionals 24 hours a day, 7 days per week, and can travel to
your location. They will come out to schools, homes, and
even to parks, malls, or parking lots. If the crisis unit
determines that the individual is at high risk for harm, they
will transport the individual to the hospital. Usually the
goal is to try to keep the person out of the hospital by
arranging crisis counseling and implementing a safety plan
at home. However, this is not always an option.

Once at the hospital, usually a psychiatric nurse or
crisis intervention specialist evaluates the safety risk. If it
is high, then the hospital staff will hold the individual as a
safety precaution and treatment intervention. The hospital staff will refer to this as a "72-hour hold" or a "5150"
(California Welfare and Institution Code, Section 5150).
An individual is held for 72 hours so that she can be
assessed for continued safety risk or suicidal ideation/
intent. If, after 72 hours, the individual is assessed to be

safe (no longer a risk to herself or others) then she is released. If her safety status has not changed (still at risk for harming herself), then she will be placed on another hold called a "5250." This process continues as long as the person is in danger of harming herself. It is likely that the individual will be transported and admitted to a psychiatric hospital before beginning her 72 hour hold. These hospitals have trained professionals to work with adolescents in crisis.

It is important for parents to help their child understand that being held in the hospital is not a form of punishment. Insinuating that it is a punishment often worsens their negative feelings about themselves and heightens the risk of self-injury. It should be clear that the hospital stay is a temporary treatment intervention focused on safety. It should be viewed as a loving, caring, and supportive environment for a person who is suffering.

Along the same lines, parents should never threaten to send their child to a hospital for "misbehaving." These threats are problematic for a few reasons. First, they create the impression that the hospital is a place of punishment. Second, a person will never be admitted to a hospital for misbehaving. The requirements for admittance are very specific and clear. A person will be admitted if they are at suicidal, homicidal or gravely disabled (meaning due to a mental disorder, the person cannot take care of even her own personal basic needs, i.e, food, clothing, shelter). Third, and perhaps most importantly, these kinds of threats make a child feel like they are a burden, and that their parents are trying to get rid of them. This leads to feelings of shame, guilt, hopelessness, and overwhelming sadness.

Sara was 13 years old when her mother asked her if she was suicidal. Her parents were aware of their daughter's self-injurious past. Sara used to scratch her arms a few times a week when she was stressed out. This went on for approximately three months before she entered treatment. More recently, Sara's parents noticed that she had fresh cuts on her shins. Sara told them that she fell walking up a flight of stairs at school. Her parents wanted to believe her since, to their knowledge, she had not harmed herself in over six months. However, something was different about their daughter this time. Sara was not eating or sleeping well. She was isolating herself from her friends and she was irritable with all family members. In the past, even when Sara engaged in self-injurious behavior, she seemed happy. In fact, her parents had no idea she was cutting herself until they got a call from her teacher. This time Sara's mood was different. She seemed deeply depressed and her mother was certain that something was very wrong.

At first, Sara denied having any suicidal ideation. She told her mother that she was "in a bad mood" and asked to be left alone. Her mother was not convinced by her denial of suicidal feelings and re-approached her. She knew that self-injury was typically not an indicator of suicidal intent, but she also knew that her daughter could be self-injuring and suicidal at the same time.

Sara's mother followed her instincts. She told Sara that if she was feeling distressed, she wanted to help. Sara opened up to her mother and told her the truth. She admitted to suicidal ideation and having a plan to kill herself that night. Her mother immediately took her to the local emergency room where she was placed on a 72-hour safety hold. Later that night she was transferred to an adolescent psychiatric hospital where she remained for two weeks. She received daily group counseling, individual therapy, and family therapy. Sara stated, "I didn't want to be in the hospital, and every day I begged my parents to get me out, but I know it is what saved my life."

IS SELF-INJURY HIGH RISK OR LOW RISK?

For safety reasons, it is important to understand the difference between high-risk and low-risk forms of self-injurious behavior. Safety is always a concern when an individual is self-inflicting bodily harm. However, it is of the greatest concern when the risk level is high. It is imperative to intervene expediently when high-risk behavior is involved, such as in the case of the anonymous caller described previously. Deep lacerations requiring stitches, or third degree burns, are more likely to cause significant trauma or even death than superficial scratches and singed hair follicles.

There are two measures that determine whether a self-injurer is considered high risk or low risk. The first is the type of instrument they use. The second is the place on their body where they self-mutilate. Higher-risk instruments tend to include knives, razors, glass, and fire sources. Lower-risk instruments may include push pins, paperclips, staples, pencils, and rubber bands. Higher-risk body parts typically include wrists, neck, and inner thighs. Lower-risk body parts are generally forearms, upper thighs, stomach, and shoulders.

There are many consequences to higher-risk behavior. The most vital is obviously safety. However, another consequence, which is often overlooked, is scarring. Most self-injurers are left with scars on their body to indicate where they inflicted bodily harm.

Different individuals have different feelings about their scars. Some are embarrassed, some are proud, and some are indifferent. In any case, they are real and often permanent. Nadia writes, "The 400 or so scars on my body weren't meant to mock me and scream – You Are a Screw Up! Look at you – years later! But this is exactly what they do." She states, "It is ironic how the very thing that got me through is now the source of so much shame."

Conversely, Nicole relates, "I am glad I have my scars. They tell a story about my life and are reminders of the struggles I have worked hard to overcome." She is not ashamed or embarrassed about her scars and does not want them to fade. She states, "Losing my scars would be like losing a part of myself."

Joey is indifferent to his scars. He says, "I am not ashamed and I am not proud of them. They are what they are and there is nothing I can do to change that. I knew I would be marking my body every time I chose to self-injure so I don't concern myself with the scars now."

Parents have their own feelings about their child's scars. Most do not like to look at them and are devastated by what their child has done to herself. Parents often blame themselves that they let things get this far without knowledge or intervention. They worry that others will be quick to criticize, blame, and/or label if the scars are noticed. Therefore, parents often want to hide their children's scars from others.

The individual struggling with self-injury recognizes how frightened, horrified, and even disgusted their parents often are when they see the damage that they have done to their skin. They are easily able to recognize when a parent is embarassed and ashamed of their actions. Although this may be a understandable parental reaction and a predictable consequence for the person engaging in self-injurious behavior, it is extremely upsetting to the person who is struggling with the problem.

Parents often try to hide their child's problem with self-injury from others. Many are invested in keeping this a secret from others (see chapter 3 for more details). A big part of covering up the problem is covering up their child's scars. When parents go to great lengths to hide the problem from others (even when well-intentioned), it can make the individual feel worthless, unloved, and unsupported. Many of my patients report that they feel like a disappointment to their parents and that they are "not good enough" in their parents' eyes.

The following poem illustrates one patient's feelings about her scars and her parents' response to this very visible reminder of her struggles:

It wasn't what you wanted
When I pulled up my sleeves
And exposed the deeply etched wounds of my past,
Healing still, in memory.
I remember your face as you examined my flesh
You kept the disgust from your voice
but it was there in your eyes.
Still, you caressed the bitter reminders of years best forgotten:
Angry scars patterning arms still weak and frail.
With a saccharine smile you tried to reassure me
that it was okay
that you didn't mind.
But then you asked me to hide them,
embarrassed by my pathos.
I said I wouldn't have it any other way, I
pulled my sleeves down.
But now, months later, I feel used and dirty
because you with your savior complex
asked for emotional nudity
only to escape your own feelings of parental unworthiness
And to showcase your perfect daughter with no problems.

THE MOST COMMON REASONS WHY INDIVIDUALS SELF-INJURE

There are several reasons that individuals self-injure. Understanding why a person engages in the behavior is very important in order to successfully treat the problem. Listed below are common reasons that individuals self-injure.

1. To Escape Emptiness and Feel Alive

Nadia shared a mental picture with me to help me better understand the reasons behind her self-injurious behavior. She asked me to imagine a large airy room with sparse furniture and big, wood-framed windows that were open and letting in the soft sounds of birds. In this room, the early morning sun was shining through the open windows and the lace curtains were gently blowing in the breeze. The plaster walls were plain and white, their expanse interrupted only by an occasional ladder back chair standing nearby. The floors were rustic with wide, planked wood. There was only one door leading into the room and it was closed. In the center of the room, bathed in sunlight, was a simple, small wood table with only one object on its surface, a beautiful, cut crystal bud vase holding a single rose. The rose was just beginning to open.

As I followed Nadia's description, the sunlit, serene feel of the room turned suddenly grey and foreboding when she told me that the entire scene was in black and white, like an old movie. She said that the rose was the only color present and it was strikingly red. "The rose is so red, that when I see it in my mind, I can feel my heart beat, like a passion simmering underneath my skin," she said. Nadia continued the narrative, noting that as she looked at the rose more closely, she noticed beads of moisture on its delicate petals. She touched these drops of moisture, and they felt unexpectedly warm. When she looked down at her fingertips, she saw blood. "My blood is the tiny droplets on that rose and it is just as crimson as the flower," she says.

Nadia wanted to feel the warmth of her blood in the midst of her cold, grey world. She wanted to see color again. She wanted to feel again. She says, "I want my passion for life to return. I want it to flow out of me, instead of being buried so deep inside that I am beginning to wonder if it is there anymore. I want to feel warm and red, not cold and grey."

Nadia eloquently illustrates one of the most frequently cited reasons for self-injurious behavior. She self-mutilates to *feel* alive and to escape the emptiness she experiences in her daily life. It is common for individuals to comment that they do not "feel real or human," and that the pain they elicit along with the sight of blood flowing from their body creates a sense of "being alive." If this seems confusing, think about all the people you know who go to great lengths to "feel alive" or "feel young and energetic."

In trying to describe this concept to others, I often share an example from the movie, *Titanic*. Envision the scene where Leonardo DiCaprio climbs up on the ship's most forward railing. With the wind blowing in his face and only water beneath him, he stands up with his hands raised high up into the air and yells "I'm the King of the World!" This is a wonderful depiction of an individual who is experiencing a sense of "feeling and being alive." Self-injurers strive to create this experience through their acts of bodily harm. Because they often do not believe that they can achieve this feeling without self-injury, they develop a pattern of its use.

2. As Punishment

A second common reason why individuals self-injure is for punishment. Self-injurers seek to punish themselves, either for what they perceive as their own failings (internal reasons), or because of external events. Internal reasons for punishment include things like failing a test, missing the winning goal or saying something that you later regret. As a result, the person feels angry, frustrated and disappointed in themselves. For example, Brian states, "When I mess up in a game or on a test, I look for a way to punish myself. Self-injury provides me with that way."

External reasons for punishment might include a friend being rude, a fight with parents, a flight being cancelled, a car breaking down, or the weather ruining plans. As a result, the person feels angry, frustrated, and disappointed with something or someone in the outside world. Elaine explains, "A client changes his mind about a deal due to financial constraints, or it rains during my only vacation of the year, and I cannot help but turn to my trusted friend, my piece of glass. Using it during those times is a way to purge myself of all my anger and disappointment." Or, according to Sara, "When a friend at school gives me a dirty look, or talks about me behind my back, or when I get into a fight with my parents, the anger and sadness I feel is so big that I cut to deal with it."

3. TO NUMB FEELINGS

A third common reason that people self-injure is to numb uncomfortable feelings. In this case, one of two things happens. Either emotional pain is turned into physical pain because it is easier to deal with, or the person masters numbing the physical pain which in turn helps them to achieve their ultimate goal of relieving their emotional pain. In either case, however, the same goal is achieved. The emotional pain is managed by finding a way to numb it or avoid it completely.

Joey exemplifies this point. He expresses his pain physically by burning. He comments, "I do not like the sight of blood or the way it feels to slice my skin. Cutting causes me too much pain, so I burn instead." Joey does not self-injure to feel pain. He self-injures to numb pain. He states, "I can numb the burning sensation on my arms or legs whenever I put a lighter or cigarette to my skin. I like the power and control I feel when I make the pain go away." For Joey, mastery over physical pain is followed by mastery over emotional pain.

4. TO DECREASE TENSION

The last common reason that people self-injure is to decrease tension and stress. This is one of the most prevalent indicators for self-injurious behavior and the one cited most often when patients first come into my office. Many of my patients are struggling with intense pressure and stress in their lives. During the initial intake interview, these patients often admit to utilizing self-injury as a way to relieve those feelings. I hear statements like "It calms me down," "It relieves tension," or "I feel at peace with myself when I do it."

This calming technique, although very unhealthy, seems to work in the short term. The problem is that it does not work in the long term and can lead to very dangerous consequences. Aside from the reasons behind self-injurious behavior, the behavior itself can be highly detrimental both physically and psychologically. However, when used to relieve tension and stress, there is an added component which makes it more dangerous and potentially lethal.

In my professional experience, I have found that there is a significant correlation between increasing tension and increasing severity of the self-injurious behavior. In other words, the more stress and tension that the individual feels, the greater the severity of the self-injurious act. As discussed above, it is not uncommon for these patients to end up in the hospital because their behavior becomes so dangerous and out of control.

For example, Kathy was admitted to the hospital following an incident of self-injurious behavior where she cut so deep that she stated, "I even scared myself." She explained, "I needed to cut more deeply to get the same effect. The tension I was feeling was so powerful that superficial cutting did not seem to get rid of all my stress. I needed something more." Nadia found herself in a similar situation. She was hospitalized right before a family reunion. She cut so deep, she could see bone. She did not want to go to the hospital, but knew that it was what she needed. She was afraid that she would take things too far as a way to try to get the relief she was looking for. She stated, "The cuts I made on a daily basis were not enough. I needed something more. It was like I built up a tolerance to the pain and couldn't get the same feeling unless I dug deeper into my skin."

5. A COPING MECHANISM

In summary, self-injurious behavior is a coping mechanism. As defined, it is a way for individuals to manage overwhelming feelings that are too painful or difficult to verbalize. The first step in helping a loved one who is self-injuring is understanding her pain and recognizing that she is attempting to manage it. The remainder of this book will focus on identification of self-injury as well as prevention and intervention. Specific guidelines and techniques that can help self-injurers learn to manage painful emotions in a way that is safer, healthier, and more productive will be addressed.

3

IDENTIFYING SELF-INJURY

"Cutting became my cry for help when words could not do it for me. I don't think I would have stopped if my coach hadn't noticed. She picked up on the warning signs and identified the problem. Only then did I get the help I so desperately needed but could not ask for."
- Jessica, age 15

Perhaps you are reading this chapter because your teen self-injures, or maybe you know someone else that does. Maybe you are reading it because you have suspicions that your child is engaging in self-harming behaviors. In any case, I would like to applaud your willingness to examine the problem and identify the severity of your child's situation. With self-injury is becoming as wide-spread as substance abuse and eating disorders, it is not uncommon for most people to know someone who struggles with this problem. Yet parents generally have little information as to what they can do to help. The first step is identifying the problem and simply acknowledging that it exists.

In the past 18 years, I have worked with more individuals who self-injure than I can count. What was once thought of as a teenage phenomenon is now recognized as a struggle faced by individuals of all ages. It may surprise you to know that the incidence of habitual bodily harm is approximately 1% in our country. With a reported 2 million cases in the United States alone, it is clear that this disorder has become rampant and affects a diverse population. This number is growing at a fast rate and there is evidence it is beginning to occur among younger and younger individuals.

While some of the individuals that have walked into my office have been as young as nine, it is still more common among teenagers. If left untreated, this behavior often continues into adulthood. In addition, the longer the individual struggles with the problem, the harder it is likely to be for them to stop the behavior. Therefore, getting help as soon as possible is very important. This is a serious problem that should be treated aggressively when first identified.

WARNING SIGNS

There are several signs that may indicate an individual is engaging in self-injurious behavior. One of the biggest red flags is when the individual always wears long sleeves and pants, even when the weather is warm. Another red flag is frequently unexplained or justified injuries such as scratches, cuts or burns. Amber recalls how she attempted to hide her self-harm from people at school. She states, "My solution was long sleeves and pants, and at soccer practice I cleverly used a sock which I said was a sweat band." In addition, she remembers having to explain why she had scratches on her body. "I made up crazy stories about my cat to answer some of the questions," she recalls.

Other warning signs include low self-esteem, a feeling of being easily overwhelmed, difficulty maintaining stable, healthy relationships, and trouble functioning at school, home or work. Although all of these factors may be symptoms, they are not, in and of themselves, direct indicators that self-injurious behavior is present.

PARENT CHECKLIST - PHYSICAL SIGNS

1. Does my child have unexplained scratches, bruises, burns, or cuts?
2. If my child has scratches, are they linear?
3. If my child has burns, are they the same shape, e.g., round from a cigarette or long and thin from a hot iron?
4. Does my child avoid answering when asked where the injuries came from?

5. Does my child give vague or general reasons for her injuries, e.g., "I fell in a rose bush."
6. Does my child have words carved into her skin?
7. Does my child hide knives, razors, glass, bent paper clips or any other sharp objects in her room?
8. Does my child wear long sleeves and pants in warm weather?
9. Does my child suddenly refuse to go swimming, gymnastics, wrestling, ballet or any other sport where skin will be revealed?

PARENT CHECKLIST - EMOTIONAL SIGNS

1. Does my child seem depressed?
2. Does my child have frequent and intense mood swings?
3. Is my child isolating from her friends and family?
4. Is my child less communicative with friends and family?
5. Is my child engaging in more "out of control behavior" resulting in more arguments at home?
6. Does my child call herself names, such as "ugly", "stupid," "fat," and "worthless?"

GIVING VOICE TO PAIN THAT HAS NO WORDS

Those who self-injure are desperately trying to give voice to pain that has no words. The origin of this pain is different for each individual. As mentioned in the previous chapter, these reasons may include tension reduction, self-punishment, a sense of belonging, and the desire to "feel alive" or conversely a way to "numb" their pain.

Understanding the specific reasons an individual is self-harming is essential in order to achieve a successful recovery. However, one thing that self-injurers tend to have in common is their unwillingness or inability to verbally express emotional distress. Therefore, gaining insight and knowledge about why your child engages in self-injurious behavior may not be easy. In fact, most kids are unwilling to talk about this behavior and keep it a secret, particularly from their parents.

To make matters even more complex, often self-injury is a symptom of a more serious mental illness such as Post Traumatic Stress Disorder, Borderline Personality Disorder, Major Depression or Bipolar Disorder. If this is the case, treating the underlying illness is highly recommended as it will lead to improved psychological well-being and aid in the recovery process for self-injury. However, parents will not necessarily know if there is an underlying mental health issue until their child is evaluated by a professional. This evaluation usually does not occur until there is acknowledgement of the problem.

Although self-injurious behavior is usually concealed rather than flaunted, it has received enough attention in the media to make the topic less "taboo" and therefore more frequently discussed. Perhaps these barriers were first broken down years ago when Hollywood stars such as Roseanne Barr and Johnny Depp as well as royal favorite, Princess Diana, admitted to the behavior. Fortunately, recognition of this problem has led to an increase in treatment intervention.

ACKNOWLEDGING THE PROBLEM

The first step in treatment and recovery is acknowledging that there is a problem. This is not always easy to do. Your teen may experience great confusion, guilt, and shame for her actions. Admitting that there is a problem and seeking treatment demonstrates courage and great strength. The teen can be proud of herself for taking that first step in recovery. You, as parents, can be proud that you supported your teen in doing so.

Although self-injury is much better understood today than it was in the past, it is still accompanied by myths and stereotypes. Unfortunately, admitting to the problem means risking these misconceptions. For example, the fear of being labeled "suicidal" commonly prevents admission of the problem. As discussed, for the most part, individuals who self-harm do it to cope with distressing emotions, not with the intent to commit suicide.

In addition, the fear of being referred to as a "cutter," which then follows with labels such as "psycho," "borderline," "Goth," or "emo," commonly inhibit identification of the problem. These labels often lead to disrespect and rejection from others. For example, Sarah is the senior class president at her local high school. She recently admitted self-injuring to some of her classmates. In turn, several of them questioned her leadership capability. Rhonda is the chief editor of her high school newspaper. Some of her classmates noticed the multiple scars on her forearm, and began treating her differently. One eventually asked her how many times she tried to kill herself and if she would ever hurt anyone else. When her teacher found out, he questioned her ability to perform her duties for the paper.

It is no wonder that many self-injurers hide this problem. For the same reasons, parents also often deny that a problem exists. Parents are understandably protective of their children. They certainly do not want their child to experience the pain and humiliation of a negative label as well as mistreatment from others. So they join with their child and avoid discussion of the problem.

Many parents will even go to great lengths to steer clear of topics they know are upsetting to their child, in an effort to minimize their child's distress, and make them less likely to self-harm. In this example, parental intentions are good. However, the outcomes usually are not. Attempting to help your child feel better by helping them ignore or avoid their own distressing emotions often backfires. There is no lesson in it for them. Children need to learn how to manage their distress in healthy and functional ways. Otherwise, their distress may become too difficult to ignore and eventually lead them to negative coping methods (e.g., self-injurious behaviors, eating disorders, substance abuse, violence, etc.).

Another reason parents often deny there is a problem is because they see their children's behavior as a reflection of their own parenting abilities. If you read this sentence and it stung a little, you are not alone. I know many parents who have struggled with acknowledging their child's self-harm because they worry that it will somehow signify that they have failed as parents. The reality is that self-injury is a coping mechanism and a choice. Your child needs support, understanding, and guidance to help her get back on track and away from something that can be both psychologically and medically dangerous. Her problem is not about you. It is about her.

When a parent (even unknowingly or unintentionally) makes the problem about them, it sends a negative message to the child. How do you think the child feels if they know (and they always know!) that their parent is refusing to acknowledge their problem because of their own embarrassment and shame? The answer is that it makes the child feel awful. My question to parents is this: How is your child going to be able to admit the problem and get help when they know that their own parents, the people who are supposed to love them unconditionally, cannot handle acknowledging it? Children need motivation to get better. They need love, understanding, and support. Parents can help their child find the motivation necessary to change only when they can acknowledge that something needs changing.

FINDING MOTIVATION

Once the problem is acknowledged, the next step is to find the motivation to stop. This may not be easy either since self-harm serves a purpose. First, the teen needs to understand why she is doing it and then find alternative ways to fulfill the same need. For example, if she self-injures to reduce stress, then she needs to think about healthier ways to relieve tension. The purpose of treatment is to eliminate the emotional distress the person is feeling. The possibility of finding some relief from these painful feelings can be a strong incentive to reach out for help.

This said, parents should prepare for the fact that many teens resist treatment out of fear that they will lose their coping mechanism. They are scared and unwilling to give up the one behavior that, in their mind, helps them deal with their problems. Therefore, it is important to assure them that during treatment, alternative behaviors will be explored to help relieve their distress. In addition, the unproductive thoughts that lead to the distressing emotions will be identified and challenged. The result should be an overall reduction in emotional distress, along with learning healthier, more functional coping mechanisms that can be utilized in time of need.

Seeking treatment as early as possible is vital. Getting help early leads to higher rates of success. The good news is that this is a behavior that can be stopped with help from a trained professional. Moreover, that help might ultimately change your teen's life in more positive ways than either of you might imagine.

4

PREVENTION

"I stumbled upon a poem my 13-year-old daughter was writing in her room one night. She had only written a few lines, but what they said stunned me. She wrote, 'I don't know what to do, when I sit filled with anger and stew. I don't want to die, but can barely survive. What is my way out, since I cannot shout? How about secret bleeds for my unmet needs?' I knew immediately that I had to get help for my daughter, because she was headed down a very dangerous path."

- Veronica, age 46 (mother)

EARLY DETECTION

One of the most effective ways to prevent the development of self-injurious behavior is to identify emerging symptoms early. As mentioned previously, self-injury can feel highly addictive to the person who is engaging in it. In addition, the person can escalate very quickly from lower risk to higher risk self-behavior. These two factors combined lead us to see self-injury as an aggressive problem that needs to be treated promptly (which will be discussed in detail in the treatment chapter). If parents and caregivers can recognize and respond quickly to symptoms, even though they may seem benign, there is a good possibility that this devastating problem can be stopped before it starts.

Early detection means that parents must be careful not to overlook, or minimize signs and symptoms of self-harm. While it seems ludicrous to suggest that a parent would downplay a harmful and potentially lethal problem, in my experience, it happens all the time. Parents do not do this because they are uncaring or neglectful. They do it because they are either unaware that their child is engaging in the behavior or they feel helpless to stop it.

It is not uncommon for individuals to hide this behavior and make up excuses for their wounds. Even if parents are suspicious, they want to believe these stories and deny that their child would intentionally harm herself. And if parents are clueless, they have no reason to disbelieve. Many parents have never even heard of self-mutilation, which makes the problem even harder to recognize.

Society also plays a role in parental denial. Society tells our youth that in order to be popular and successful in life, they need to look a certain way. The standards include not only weight (being thin and in shape), but also apply to skin as well. There is a relentless focus on products that get rid of acne, blemishes, wrinkles, and any other type of imperfection. Accordingly, intentionally scarring your body seems incomprehensible to most. Parents want their children to be happy and successful and to look good. Until parents are given some sort of indication that their child is self-injuring, especially if it is resulting in scars, they are usually not alarmed and thus do not intervene.

Parents are not the only ones who may brush off symptoms. In my professional experience, coaches, teachers, and even doctors have all done this. These adults also want to believe the excuses given by the kids engaging in the behavior. Coaches and teachers, like parents, want their kids (their athletes and students) to be successful. Bringing attention to self-injurious behavior is scary for them. Although identifying the problem can have positive consequences (i.e. leading to treatment and recovery), it can also have negative consequences (i.e. labels, stereotypes).

In addition, schools have been known to suspend and even expel kids who engage in self-injurious behavior. Therefore, adults working at a school are often afraid to bring this information to light because they want to protect their athlete/student from overzealous school administrators who do not understand the problem.

Several years ago, I worked with a patient who was in middle school. She brought a piece of glass to school every day and hid it in her backpack. When stressed out, she would often go into the bathroom, take out the glass, and cut herself. After months of treatment, she decided she did not need to use this negative coping mechanism any longer and replaced it with a healthier one. She was self-injury free for several months until one day, she learned that a friend had died. She was extremely distraught, and afraid that she might self-injure as a way to cope.

A friend of hers gave her a razor blade and told her that nobody would judge her if she went back to her old ways. My patient decided that she did not want to do this, and gave the razor blade to the school counselor. The school counselor relayed the story to the principal who immediately brought the girl in for questioning. Unfortunately, the principal's line of action was to suspend her immediately while waiting for an expulsion hearing. The principal explained that the school had a "no weapons" policy, that specified immediate expulsion for any student caught bringing a weapon onto campus.

I was asked to attend the expulsion hearing, along with an attorney that the family hired. At the hearing, the attorney argued that the girl's particular circumstance (bringing a weapon to school for the purpose of self-harm) did not reflect the intent of the school weapons policy. The policy was clearly designed to protect the students from assault with a weapon by other students. There was nothing in the policy that indicated immediate expulsion from school for use of a weapon on one-self. The attorney was able to address this issue and the girl was not expelled from school.

The issue that I brought up during the hearing was a little different. It is probably the topic that most of you are struggling with, as parents reading this story, because it is the most relevant to the girl's emotional and physical well-being. First, I don't think any parent can deny that it is disturbing that this girl's so-called best friend offered her a razor blade. In fact, not only did the friend offer her a weapon to use to injure her body, but offered her a justification for a potential relapse as well. My patient noted that it was as if her friend was giving her permission to slice up her body. Clearly, our hope is that our youth have best friends who lend healthy support and encouragement when in times of need, not the opposite.

Second, the other disturbing feature of this situation is that the girl got in trouble for reaching out to an adult for help. Most would agree that the girl acted admirably in this scenario despite her friend's solicitation to self-harm. She made the healthy decision to not self-injure, she turned a potentially dangerous weapon into a school offi-cial (instead of throwing it on the ground or in a garbage can for someone else to hurt themselves with), and she utilized an alternative coping mechanism (journaling her feelings about her friend's death). Despite all of this, she was suspended from school awaiting an expulsion hearing. What message does this send to our youth? Unfortunately, not the message most of us would hope for.

ASSESSING YOUR CHILD

Parents often ask me how they can assess the situation with their child. While most parents are willing to have their children attend therapy sessions if there is a diagnosed problem, some parents are uncomfortable bringing their child to treatment without being certain that there is "something wrong." They prefer to shield their child from a visit with a counselor, and any associated stigma. Actually this presents parents with a wonderful opportunity to teach their children that going to see a therapist is a helpful way for people to explore issues of concern. It can be seen as similar as going to the pediatrician for a routine check-up.

Parents who are uncomfortable bringing their child to a therapist without a formal diagnosis in place may want to consider asking their child some of the questions listed below. While these questions can help open the lines of communication, it is important to remember that a parent should never try to be their child's therapist. Many kids are not comfortable answering their parents' questions about sensitive matters. They are often much more at ease talking to an objective person who has expertise in the area.

Accordingly, my first recommendation is always that parents ask their child whether they would prefer to speak with a professional, or with the parent. If the child prefers a counselor, it usually means that they are worried about something going on in their lives, and the best thing to do is to set up an appointment for them. This answer also suggests that they are motivated to talk to someone, and when the child cooperates rather than resists, therapy is much more successful. Lastly, kids usually have great respect for their parents when they are allowed to be involved in the choice of who they see. It is empowering for them, and often leads to greater investment in therapy.

PARENT ASSESSMENT QUESTIONS

Ask the following:

1. Do you think what you are doing is considered self-injury? If so, do you feel compulsively drawn to engage in this behavior?
2. Are you cutting, carving or burning as a way to express yourself?
3. Does scratching, hitting, cutting, carving or burning yourself consume your thoughts or interfere with your ability to function normally? This includes socially, academically, and occupationally.
4. Have you ever scared yourself because you went too far?
5. Is is realistic to say that you couldn't stop scratching, hitting, cutting, or burning today, even if you wanted to?

It is very important for parents to understand that if their child answers yes to any of these questions, they should immediately seek professional consultation and assessment. Remember that an individual self-injures for a reason. A professional needs to work with your child to find out why.

Whether your child talks to you about signs and symptoms or whether you observe them yourself, it is important to remember that as a parent, you do NOT want to minimize the problem. You also do not want to tell your child to stop the behavior. Unfortunately, this does not work! If it was that simple, your child probably would stopped already, especially once she realized the physical and emotional damage it was causing.

Self-injury fulfills some need for the individual. If your child knows what that need is, and is willing to share this information with you, show your support by listening to what she has to say. Try to understand what her need is, and promote alternative behaviors that fulfill the same need in healthier ways (chapter 8). However, be careful not to permit the child to engage in other unhealthy and/ or self-injurious behaviors. For example, if your child is cutting, do not encourage her to snap rubber bands on her wrist or immerse her hand in a bucket of ice water for long periods of time.

I bring up these examples for a very important reason. Some professionals encourage and utilize these techniques with their patients. Although I understand the reasoning behind these interventions, at the end of the day, in my opinion, these methods encourage further self-harm. What these professionals are attempting to accomplish is providing an alternative tension release that will not break the skin and that will not be as harmful. In other words, they believe that the best alternative is coming up with a way to do less damage (in theory).

The problem is that these techniques are still harmful. Over the years, I have had many patients who have done a lot of damage to themselves by snapping rubber bands on their skin or keeping their hands in ice too long (risking frostbite/gangrene). The behaviors not only cause physical harm, but emotional harm as well.

First, these interventions send a message to the person that they have to DO something in order to deal with their distress. Although finding an alternative behavior to self-injury is important, it is also essential to help the person learn how to cope with their distress internally. If they cannot find the right thing to DO (something that works for them), they will continue to self-injure.

In turn, being told by a professional to use an alternative behavior that is harmful (even if it is less harmful) is disempowering. It sends a message that the person may not be able to stop self-injuring on their own without some external force. In addition, consider the issue of escalation. The self-injury will escalate when the person does not achieve the same level of relief. This escalation can be very dangerous and move the individual into the high-risk category.

When talking to your child and trying to obtain information, be careful to avoid power struggles. Remember to keep your own emotions in check. If you find yourself getting angry, frustrated, blameful, or critical, walk away and resume the conversation at another time. These types of emotions are unproductive and can actually cause your child to shut down altogether. Trust your instincts. If you believe your child has a problem, but she is not willing to talk to you or admit that there is one, don't push it. Take some time to regroup, and talk with her later.

If your child refuses to talk to you, make an appointment with an expert in the field. Experts are trained in interviewing techniques, and are skilled in getting kids to open up about their struggles. Remember that self-injury makes people sneaky, manipulative, and willing to lie. Most individuals want to keep their self-injury secret and will try anything to avoid intervention.

THE IMPORTANCE OF ROLE MODELING

A large part of prevention involves knowing what may cause or trigger the onset of an self-injury. Although some causes may not be avoidable, such as personality traits, trauma, and family problems, other triggers can be investigated and prevented. One such trigger involves parental role modeling. Parents need to understand that it is their responsibility to model frustration tolerance and healthy coping mechanisms for their children. This can be challenging for parents, especially if they have difficulty dealing with their own frustrations in healthy ways.

Kids observe adult behavior constantly, and look to us for guidance all the time. Notice I said they **LOOK** to us for guidance. Most kids don't ask for guidance from their parents or other adult role models in their lives unless they come from a family that is very communicative and open. However, just because they don't ask for guidance does not mean that they do not **OBSERVE** what the adults around them are doing.

I have had several kids tell me that when their parent(s) are stressed out, frustrated or irritable, they engage in unhealthy coping mechanisms. For example, it is not uncommon for a parent to come home from work and walk straight to the liquor cabinet in an attempt to find liquid relaxation. These parents are role modeling the need for some unhealthy external object to help them release their stress.

For many, having a drink or two after a long hard day at work does not seem unreasonable. These parents would argue that it does indeed calm them down and make them feel more at ease. Other parents are affected differently. Some parents become more agitated, depressed, or hopeless. Whatever the outcome, the person's mood is clearly affected. Kids are smart. It does not take a rocket scientist to recognize that their parents endorse the idea of doing something - even if unhealthy and potentially detrimental- to themselves to manage their distress.

While it may seem like a large leap from substance abuse to self-injury, it is not. In fact, many of the kids I work with jump from one negative coping mechanism to another (see the section on Symptom Jumping in chapter 8). If you are engaging in behaviors that illustrate dysfunctional or unhealthy coping mechanisms in an attempt decrease your distress and feel better, it is extremely likely that your child is aware of it. I cannot tell you how many kids have told me all the details of their parents' unhealthy habits. Even if these habits do not include self-injury, they still send the message to kids that it is okay to harm one's body in order to achieve some relief.

COMMUNICATING WITH YOUR CHILD: TIPS FOR PARENTS AND CAREGIVERS

Since we have spent a lot of time emphasizing the importance of communication with our kids, it is useful to discuss how to have positive and healthy discussions with them. Most child experts will advise parents to try to be open, honest and good listeners when talking with their children. What they don't say, however, is how hard that can be, especially when the child is your own and the topic is a tough one like self-injury.

Maybe, like most parents, you don't know where to start. In addition, you don't want to sound critical, rude or oblivious. I have already listed some ways for parents to approach their child when asking assessment questions. I would like to add some additional tips below. I would also like to refer you to a wonderful book called *Bodily Harm: A Breakthrough Program for Self-Injurers*, written by Karen Conterio and Wendy Lader. Their book does a brilliant job of supporting and guiding individuals and their loved ones in what they can do when their child has been diagnosed with self-injury.

Here are some additional tips offered by our national experts for parents when talking with your child following determination that they have a problem with self-injury.

1. A caregiver should be calm and non-judgmental when talking about self-injury. This does not mean that the caregiver should not acknowledge the damaging and dangerous nature of the behavior, but it does mean that the way in which this message is conveyed should not make the child feel rejected, scolded or criticized.

2. The ideal caregiver should be firm, open-minded and empathetic. A non-judgmental attitude toward the child and her behavior must be maintained at all times. Anything other than a neutral stance will inevitably lead to reduced success in recovery.

3. Spouses must be on the same page. Present as a united front. If one caregiver says one thing and the other says another, self-injury can increase and escalate.

4. Lend support – do not hesitate to help your child fight again the negative thoughts that lead to the self-injurious behavior. *Note: it does not work to fight against your child; it does work to fight against the problem. Also do not hesitate to encourage or suggest alternative behaviors (e.g. go for a walk with your child, go to the movies, etc.).

5. The greatest resource for your child is YOU!!! Don't minimize the amount of influence you have over your child.

6. Help your child stop utilizing negative coping mechanisms. Reinforce positive ones as well as the use of internal coping mechanisms. However, this cannot be done in a critical way. Use words that focus on the problem, not on the child being the problem.

7. Help your child see that she is more than her problem with self-injury. Helping her understand and see that her identity is separate from self-injury is paramount. It is hard to fight against yourself; it is much easier to fight against a behavior.

There is one final concept to consider when communicating with your child about self-injury. While you can be empathetic, it is important to acknowledge that you may never be able to feel exactly what she is feeling. The poem below, written by an adolescent to her parents, illustrates the difference between parental understanding versus personal knowledge of self-injury. Although the writer genuinely appreciates her parents' attempts to understand what she is going through, she realizes that they will never truly be able to know what it is like to be someone who self-injures.

> *There's a difference between scratching the surface*
> *and cutting to the bone.*
> *A difference between understanding*
> *and really knowing what it's like to be trapped*
> *in a nightmare that was never a dream.*
> *And so I can tell you that there is a difference*
> *between letting you in and breaking the skin;*
> *A difference between spoken word and poetry;*
> *Between expression and attention;*
> *Between survival and denial;*
> *Between you and me.*

5

SOCIETAL INFLUENCES

"There is a lot of pressure from society to look a certain way, act a certain way, and achieve great things in life. It is all unrealistic - the bar is set completely out of reach. If society says we need to achieve the unachievable in order to be popular, successful, and content in our lives, then society has set us up for failure and disappointment."
- Candice, age 21

As mentioned in previous chapters, society plays a role in the development of self-harm. American society, more so than many other nationalities, has several defining features that support the development and maintenance of self-injurious behavior. I have created a list of these below. Many of the ideas listed come from Karen Con-

terio and Wendy Lader's book, *Bodily Harm: A Breakthrough Program for Self-Injurers* (Hyperion, 1986).

IMMEDIATE GRATIFICATION

We currently live in a society that focuses on immediate gratification. Increasingly, our culture emphasizes a
"quick fix" to even the smallest problem. This means that
we are raising our children in an environment that encourages a lack of patience.

Let's think about this for a moment. For most of us,
taking the time to prepare a home-cooked meal often does
not occur when we are busy and harassed and quite honestly, hungry. Fast food restaurants provide a quick fix solution. Unfortunately, they also foster childhood obesity.
Still, most parents would agree that it is very easy to go to
a drive-through, fast-food window and feed the whole
family in less than ten minutes. And most of the time, we
don't even wait until we get home to start eating.

I am certain that if the adult driving the car was questioned about the reason for beginning dinner in the car,
instead of waiting until the whole family was sitting
together around the dinner table, they would say that they
were hungry, hit all the red lights, and half the family was
off doing other things so they wouldn't be eating together
anyway. Doesn't this further illustrate the point? We are
becoming increasingly impatient because we expect
immediate gratification. How many of us have sat at those
endless red lights and felt like we might scream if we hit
even one more on the way home?

If this particular example doesn't resonate for you, and illustrate how we are becoming more impatient due our desire for immediate gratification, then think about this. Television commercials have become too long for us. Tivo and My DVR were created so that we could skip through commercials and watch a whole program and several others (sometimes at the same time) in a shortened period of time. Does anyone watch live television anymore? According to our teens, not many of them do.

Along the same lines, our teens also report that when they have a feeling that is uncomfortable for them, they seek to fix it immediately through some action or behavior. This is true for adults as well, who are modeling these types of behaviors for our youth. Think about the anxious or depressed individual who reaches for an over-the-counter pill, alcoholic drink or bag of chips. Although this behavior doesn't address the reason the person is feeling anxious or depressed, it does make the individual feel better, at least initially. Soon, however, the individual begins to feel guilty about the behavior, and a bad feeling replaces the good one. These bad feelings that follow can lead to the development of self-injurious behavior.

Unfortunately, many individuals, including our youth, view this type of "quick fix" or immediate gratification as positive and healthy. I suppose in some cases, it could be. After all who wants to experience back pain when it can be quickly remedied by taking two Motrin. However, it is not always that simple. For example, what if the Motrin does not work fast enough or is not strong enough to take away *all* the pain? In this case, the person might go to

their doctor and request a stronger pain medicine to achieve a "quick fix." The "quick fix" may become an addiction because the person starts to pop the pills like candy in
an attempt to avoid *all* pain.

This is similar in the case of self-harm. Remember our
discussion on escalation in an earlier chapter. If the individual attempts to avoid *all* pain and their initial attempts
(e.g., scratching with a paper clip) stop achieving that,
then she will make additional attempts using higher-
risk methods (e.g., cutting with a razor blade).

Another one of the main reasons that avoiding all
pain isn't always beneficial is that we are training our kids
to have a very low tolerance for distress. When a person
has a low tolerance for distress, ordinary events cause
them to experience greater frustration than other people
might experience. This frustration feels intolerable to
them, and leads to a search for a coping mechanism (e.g.,
cutting) that will immediately relieve their discomfort.

As you can see, this becomes a vicious cycle. Therefore, one of the ways that parents can help their children is
to model positive ways of dealing with distress. This starts
with parents allowing their child to actually feel distress.
Unfortunately, in society today, parents often work diligently to help their child avoid all pain and discomfort. As
a result, the child has no understanding of how to manage
her pain and help herself. Below is an example of how this
can play out for a child.

Years ago, I was asked to come in to provide conflict
resolution to a group of parents. These parents had their
children on the same pee wee soccer team. The kids were

all around five and six years old. The season ended and the parents had to decide whether they were going to give their kids trophies. The team was in last place because it had lost every game. Half the parents wanted to give the children on the team trophies and the other half of the parents did not.

The half that advocated for trophies made a very compelling argument. They stated that the kids tried really hard all season long and that they deserved to be rewarded for their efforts. The parents who did not want to award trophies also made a compelling argument. They stated that although the kids did try hard, they lost. In fact, not only did they lose, they came in very last place because they didn't win a single game. These parents strongly believed that when a person loses, they should not be rewarded with a prize because this is not representative of what happens in real life.

Learning how to lose gracefully is one of life's hardest lessons, and these parents wanted to teach their children this lesson early. They felt very strongly about *not* rewarding their child for coming in last place. The first set of parents agreed that it is important to learn how to lose gracefully, but they did not think pee wee soccer (at the age of five) was the necessary time and place to learn it. Instead, they wanted to come from a place of love and caring for their young children. They knew that if their child did not receive a trophy, and their child's friends on the opposing teams did, their child would be upset and disappointed. To avoid this type of feeling, they wanted to give the kids trophies.

I think most people would agree that parents intuitively want their children to feel good. No parent wants to see their child upset and hurting. However, this is part of life. So what is the right answer? You will have to decide for yourself. I can understand both sides of the argument, and shared my views with the parents during the conflict resolution session. In the end, the parents agreed to disagree, and each individual family made a personal choice as to whether or not they would give their child a trophy.

However, I did take some time to discuss how we as parents tend to "rescue" our children from their own distress. I noted that, although well-intentioned, this is not always the best thing to do for our youth. Our kids need to learn how to deal with their own distress. If we continue to provide "quick fix" solutions for them, they will follow our lead later in life and seek immediate gratification every time they encounter feelings of anger, frustration, stress or sadness. As we have already learned, this lowers our frustration tolerance, and before long our kids will feel that they cannot deal with any distressing emotion.

Going back to the pee wee soccer team, I also talked with the parents about how they could best support their child through their feelings of hurt and disappointment. I explained to all of the parents that if a child is upset or frustrated, it is important for them to talk to them about their feelings and teach them how to cope with the hurt they are experiencing. I recommended giving the kids specific examples of times when the parents as adults have been disappointed, and explaining how they felt and what they did to get through it. This is not something that all children automatically know how to do. They need adults to model this for them and help them learn to do the right thing.

If kids do not learn healthy coping mechanisms early in life, they are more apt to seek unhealthy ones later on. Self-injury is just one possibility. For a "quick fix," they may also use drugs to numb their pain or restrict their food to gain some sort of control over their life. (For more information on substance abuse and eating disorders please reference the books *What Every Parent Needs to Know About Substance Abuse* and *What Every Parent Needs to Know About Eating Disorders*, Fastpencil.com).

DISENFRANCHISED YOUTH

The second cultural influence that underscores self-injurious behavior is the fact that our society is becoming increasingly disenfranchised. Conterio and Lader illustrate how extended family members are less available to our youth, particularly in middle-to-upper class Caucasian families, where self-harm may be most prevalent. The collapse of the extended family, and the increasing isolation of the individual, means that children have fewer confidantes in times of difficulty. With more parents working outside the home, children are being raised by strangers rather than family members. Once they outgrow daycare, baby sitters and nannies take over and latchkey children become the norm.

As they become teenagers, our kids are raising themselves, looking for answers and guidance from their equally clueless peers. What do you think teens tell each other about stress management and tension release? Usually not information about sufficient sleep, proper nutrition, and adequate exercise, all of which can actually help with the problem. Instead, they discuss the ways that they relieve their own stress, which may include high-risk behaviors that can have detrimental outcomes.

While self-injury is only one of many possibilities, with this phenomenon on the rise, I am finding that more teens begin to inflict harm after learning about it from a friend.   The more distraught an individual is, the more motivated she is to find ways to release her distress. These methods can be healthy or unhealthy. If she has found an unhealthy coping mechanism such as self-injury, then she is more likely to turn to this when she is feeling "bad."

Let's go back to the decline of the family dinners. In the past, family dinners were considered a sacred event. It was important to have everyone gathered around the table at the same time to share a meal. The family dinner was the one time that family members could talk about their day and experience true feelings of togetherness. Unfortunately for many families, this ritual does not seem to exist anymore. Someone in the family is inevitably working late or at sports practice or at a music lesson. Some kids are lucky to even sit down to a meal with their siblings and a nanny. This type of fragmented family dinner often leaves kids without a good model for healthy communication. This is particularly true if kids are eating alone, or on the run.

Dinner table conversation may not seem that important to some reading this book. However, I believe it is a wonderful way for the entire family to connect. Kids learn how to communicate and gain support from their family unit each time they sit down and converse with one another. This can happen in other forums as well. For example, many parents tell me that they love the time they spend with their child in the car. It gives them the opportunity to talk about the day and any problems or struggles they may be having. Regular opportunities for open communication are essential to building family cohesion and support systems.

While all conversations adults have with children are important, since this book is on self-injury, I will focus on the importance of providing a forum for kids to discuss their thoughts, feelings, struggles, and stressors. Conterio and Lader point out that the modern teen may grow up relying very little on verbal expression to communicate their thoughts and feelings. Instead, the teen may depend more on *doing* than on *saying*. Self-injury is often used as a way to *do* something or *show* someone something rather than *saying or telling* someone something verbally. "I will *show* you how much I despise my body by carving the word 'ugly' into my thigh. I will *show* you how out of control I feel by burning my skin 'every time I screw something up.'"

DYSFUNCTIONALITY: THE NEW COOL

The third cultural influence that supports the development of unhealthy coping mechanisms among our youth is that our society is becoming a nation of addicts and "a-holics." Many would argue that self-injury fits into this category. Conterio and Lader point out that it has become "in" to be considered dysfunctional. In fact, it has become so "in" that individuals volunteer to share their dysfunction with millions of viewers on national television. Think about how many people volunteer to share their dysfunctional lives on the *Oprah Winfrey Show* and how many individuals are willing to share their problems with the entire nation on the *Dr. Phil Show*. Many of our youth are hungry for attention; so hungry that they would prefer negative attention to no attention at all. Interestingly, when it comes to self-harm, there are two different outcomes. There are the teens who hide it from everyone, seeking to avoid any type of attention for their behavior, and the teens who exploit the problem as a means to receive negative attention from almost everyone around them.

The teens in the latter example use self-injury in a manipulative way to get what they want. This is the teen girl who tells her boyfriend that she is going to cut herself if he breaks up with her. Because he is afraid she will do it, he doesn't break up with her. It is the teen boy who tells his parents if they do not let him go to the concert with his friends on Saturday night, he will burn himself. Out of fear, his parents comply. It is the individual who walks into a group therapy session bleeding from fresh wounds on her arm and tells the group she needs to talk because she has had a bad day. The group members assent and she dominates the group therapy session.

These scenarios will be revisited when we discuss intervention in a later chapter. However, I would like to briefly note something about them here. Although these negative attention-seeking behaviors are meant to get the individual what they want, they serve another purpose as well.

It is important for us to remember that individuals who self-harm often do not have the same ability as others to verbally express their pain. Therefore, they have to *show* you or *threaten to show* you the pain that they are experiencing. This is their attempt to get their needs met. For example, I have no doubt that the girl who sliced up her arms before entering group therapy needed to check in about her day. Instead of trying to communicate this verbally, she decided to show the group members the state of distress that she was in.

EMPHASIS ON THE SUPERFICIAL

Another cultural influence that contributes to the growing incidence of self-harm in our nation is that we live in a relentlessly body-focused culture where appearances are all-important and where we are encouraged by cultural imperatives to remain "on the surface of things." Researchers agree that adornment and decoration of the body are the primary means of self-expression for most cultures. Although many societies are well known for this (i.e., African Tribal societies), Western society is no different. Think about how our media is saturated with commercials advertising how we can feel better about ourselves by changing our shape, diet, scent, face or bone structure (through plastic surgery), hair color, skin color (tanning) or fashion, or by buying lotion, creams and ointments to enhance our beauty. This inevitably makes individuals, especially impressionable teenagers, feel that they are not good enough.

The media plays a role in this too. Most ads in magazines are extremely body-focused. Photoshopped models look thin and flawless, creating a complete misconception for our youth about what human beings actually look like in real life. In addition, our kids are watching movies featuring beautiful actors and actresses and wishing they could look just like them. They are usually unaware that many of these movie stars use body doubles to make them look better on the big screen. What is the old saying? The camera adds 15 pounds. Let's not forget about television and TV commercials. These forms of media also focus on physical beauty, and insinuate that you will be happier if your skin is flawless and you are movie star thin.

What if our impressionable youth cannot compete with these high standards? They inevitably feel terrible about themselves and beat themselves up (literally) for their imperfections. Unfortunately, self-injury is just one way that our youth express disgust with their bodies. Eating disorders are another. Our youth will go to great lengths to express their fear, anger, and frustration with themselves and their bodies.

Lader and Conterio explain that as long as human beings have existed, they have used the skin to communicate identity, status and any number of other characteristics such as political preference, sexual orientation, etc. These symbolizations of the self are advertised through body art – tattoos, piercing, cutting – much like a bumper sticker on a car. The scars from self-injury are also an advertisement. If asked, many of these individuals would probably state that the scars memorialize difficulties they experienced in their lives. One of my patients called it her "road map of despair." It is not uncommon for individuals to explain what individual scars represent, for example one for their parents' divorce, one for their grandmother's death, one for the loss of championship game, and so on.

Many cultures, both primitive and modern, have used tribal markings to unite their community and imbue a sense of belonging (e.g., Hindu women: red dot; Native American tribes: facial decorations, markings; street gangs: tattoos, colors). For the individual struggling with self-injury, their scars provide something similar. Unfortunately, in the more extreme cases of self-harm involving injecting toxins into the body, amputation, or unintentional suicide, the self-injurer's tribal markings can be lethal.

ADVANCES IN TECHNOLOGY

With growing technology and use of the internet, our teens communicate with their peers in numerous ways that provide instantaneous feedback. They talk and text on their cell phones, they video chat online, and they post messages and blogs on their social networking sites. Often, this technology is used in beneficial ways. For example, technology allows an individual who is strug-gling to gain immediate reinforcement. Helplines and/or chatrooms make assistance available 24/7 for the person

who is about to cut or burn and needs someone to intervene. This type of instant support is invaluable when the
urges are strong and the person does not want to relapse.

Another, often positive application of technology
involves web forums and sites such Facebook, MySpace,
LiveJournal, and Xanga, which are extremely popular
among our teens. They provide support through
online groups, which are especially valuable to individuals
who are isolating from friends and family and feel like they
have nobody to turn to. For these teens, online social networking is often the only social contact and therapeutic
support system that they have. Not surprisingly, research
shows it is much more common for females to join these
groups (chat rooms) than males.

The example above illustrates that technology is not
necessarily a bad thing. However, it can also be used negative ways that can be harmful. For example, technology
can be used to justify and maintain self-injurious
behavior. This occurs when a teen visits online sites that
encourage and support self-injury, or other destructive
behaviors. Advocating for a problem that literally causes
self-harm is ludicrous, I know. However, these sites exist
and are accessible with the click of a mouse.

As a parent, it is helpful to talk with your child about
their use of technology. Parents often believe their child
will not be honest with them if they are visiting sites that
do not support treatment and recovery. This if often true,
as kids can be very secretive about their computer use.
However, there are the exceptions, especially when the
child wants to explain the ways in which other people are

justifying the problem in an attempt to convince their parents that what they are doing is "no big deal."

If your child is trying to persuade you that this behavior is acceptable, the best thing to do is to let your child know that you are sorry that others are encouraging or justifying the self-harming behavior. Explain that it your desire and hope that she finds alternative ways to cope with her distress. Let her know that you love her and would never want her to intentionally harm herself in any way. You can also let her know that you would really like her to talk to a therapist about this if she is not already in therapy.

If she is already in treatment, encourage her to bring up peer influence at her next appointment. Often the parents of my patients tell their child that they will be contacting me directly regarding this matter to ensure that it is discussed in session. Acknowledgement of this type of peer influence opens the door for a wonderful discussion between your child and her therapist regarding readiness and motivation to stop the behavior. Remember, many kids resist entering treatment and have low motivation for recovery.

Whether your child is open or secretive about their use of technology in regard to self-injury, I encourage parents to educate themselves about the various sites their children are visiting. Most of them are public sites, which means that anyone can view their content. Additionally, if you are worried about your child, try typing her name into a search engine. You may be surprised by the information you find. You can also check your child's computer history to see what sites she has visited. Talking with your

child and encouraging open and honest communication is
always preferable. However, if you are worried for your
child's safety, you can put technology to work for you and
investigate.

INCREASED PRESSURE

Our society is changing. With more demands being
placed on our youth now than ever before, it is harder to
be a kid. Topping the list is the increased academic pressure. With a nationwide push to get into colleges, teens
feel intense pressure to excel. Getting in to top schools
requires shouldering a heavy load of advanced courses and
maintaining a high GPA. It also means participating in
sports, clubs, community service and other leadership
opportunities. These obligations come on top of the ordinary, and already significant challenges teens confront,
including friend and relationship issues, family dynamics,
body concerns, sexuality, and holding down some sort of
job. The result is that kids that used to face daily challenges with anticipation increasingly feel out of control
and overwhelmed.

The ever-increasing pressures placed on our youth
today drive them to more severe emotional extremes than
ever before. The rising tension and distress related to academic expectations has created what has been
described as a "silent epidemic" in our schools, in which
students are stressed out, depressed, and disengaged. Our
teens are looking for ways to relieve this stress. They find
different outlets, some which are positive such as sports,

music, and art, and some that are negative, including eating problems, substance abuse, sex, and self-injury.

INCREASED DESIRE FOR STIMULATION

One last societal influence that needs to be considered is our increased desire for stimulation. We have talked at length about how individuals are searching for a way to feel good. In addition, they are constantly looking for a cure to boredom. Teens are looking for excitement. We have created a society that focuses on highly stimulating things. Unfortunately, self-injury is one of those things.

As we have already discussed, many teens report that they engage in self-injurious behavior as a way to feel alive. They also report engaging in self-injurious behavior to alleviate boredom. In fact, they say it is the perfect cure to the combination of the two. This may surprise you to hear, but it is true. This is not to say that just anybody will engage in self-injurious behavior as a way to self-stimulate and cure boredom. However, once someone has tried it, it is often the reason they continue to engage in this behavior. In addition, it is one of the reasons that escalation of the behavior occurs.

Self-injury is not the only way that our youth seek stimulation and cure boredom in unhealthy ways. They may also drink, use drugs, gamble, have sex, watch pornography, street race, get into physical fights, play chicken, etc. Clearly all of these outlets have a high potential for dire consequences. However, adolescents believe they are invincible and therefore, do not think about them.

Instead, they continue to engage in these behaviors in order to experience a "rush" of adrenaline.

Everything seems to need to be more stimulating for our youth these days.   Athletic sports are a prime example. Recent studies illustrate that kids favor high-action sports, like soccer and basketball, over slower ones like baseball and ballet. Baseball has the highest drop-out rate of any sport in the past decade. Many of our kids are bored with it and no longer view it as a favorite American pastime. My kids play baseball currently, and it is not uncommon for me to hear a kid standing in the outfield say "This is boring!" or "How much longer till the game is over?"

There has been a similar shift in the kind of movies our kids enjoy. Has anyone noticed how bored our five-to-seven-year-olds have become watching old Disney movies? Although adorable and classic, these movies do not have fast-paced, exciting chase scenes, 3D, or other stimulating special effects. As a result, they often seem boring to kids.

The recent addition of D-Box has advanced this trend even further by making the movie experience physically as well as visually stimulating.   These specialized seats actually move, so that the viewer feels as though they are in the airplane that is diving towards the ground, or speeding in a safari jeep across a rough African plain. As advertised, these stimulators take the cinematic experience to the next level.

As our kids get older, we continue to see this problem. For example, let's look at the change in how movies and television shows are rated. What is now rated PG -13 would have been rated R when we were kids. This is not only due to the graphic content such as self-injury, eating disorders or substance abuse in the movie, but also due to the sex, violence and adult language in the show.

Kids have little downtime between the increase in their school work and homework load, their sports schedules, and afterschool activities. This lack of free time is not healthy; however, it is what most kids have become accustomed to. When kids are not busy, they become bored. Just as our kids are *not* being taught how to deal with distressing emotions, they are *not* being taught how to deal with boredom.

Our kids do not know how to appreciate downtime. In fact, many of them feel uneasy and even guilty when they are relaxing. This in part may be due to what is being modeled for them. If the important role models in their lives view relaxation as laziness, then they will adopt this belief system for themselves.

There is no doubt that most of us have very busy lifestyles. This has changed over the years and is true for more families now than ever before. However, in our busy lives, it is important to learn how to unwind. If we as adults can do this, then we can teach it to our children. Don't we all want our children to appreciate moments of quiet and relaxation?

"If our American way of life fails the child, it fails us all."
- Pearl S. Buck

6

OVERCOMING RESISTANCE AND ENTERING TREATMENT

"Some of the greatest battles will be fought within the silent chambers of your own soul."
- Ezra Taft Benson

Different people have different responses to therapy and treatment. Some are resistant to counseling and some are highly motivated to change. When Susie walked into my office for the first time, I could immediately tell she was not happy about being there. She was 14 years old, casually dressed, and very quiet. She did not make eye contact with me, or with her parents, who had accompanied her to the initial intake appointment. When I asked Susie how she thought I might be able to help her, she snapped, "I don't want any help. I don't have a problem!

My parents forced me to come." Conversely, Morgan
entered therapy in a very different way. She drove herself
to the appointment and attended the initial intake session
alone. She was 17, and highly motivated for therapy.
Before I could say a word, she began informing me of her
desire to "get well."

EXPLAINING THAT TREATMENT IS MANDATORY

Finding a good fit with the therapist is imperative in
achieving success. While your child may help choose a
particular therapist based on whether he or she feels comfortable (see information about this below), kids struggling with self-injury should **never** have a choice about
attending treatment. Parents should make it very clear to
their child that they must be involved in some type of
therapeutic intervention.

It is appropriate to explain to your child why she has no
choice in this matter. Explain that you love her and that
you are very concerned for both her physical and mental
well-being. Tell her that without treatment, you are afraid
that her self-injurious behavior will increase in both frequency and intensity, which in some cases can lead to
unintentional death. Tell her firmly that you are NOT
going to let that happen because part of your job as a
parent is keeping your child safe. Tell her that it would be
neglectful and uncaring for you to allow her to avoid treatment intervention.

To help make this last premise clear to children, I suggest that parents use the following analogy:

"If I found out you were doing drugs every day, I would not sit around and do nothing about it; if I found out that you were binging and purging every day, I would not sit around and do nothing about it.; and if I found out that you were sick with the swine flu, I would not sit around and do nothing about it. In all of these cases, it would be ludicrous for me **not** to set up an appointment with a doctor and begin some sort of treatment immediately. Self-injury is not that different from these other conditions. It is a serious problem that needs to be treated aggressively. Therefore, I am not going to wait and see if things get better on their own. I love you and care about you too much to let anything bad happen to you."

After hearing these things from their parent(s), most kids will begin therapy, even if begrudgingly. While this discussion will not cause your child to jump for joy, and suddenly be wildly motivated to get well, these words are usually very meaningful for kids. In fact, they are often remembered and discussed later in treatment. However, in that initial moment, they will never admit it to you.

SPECIFIC STRATEGIES TO OVERCOMING RESISTANCE

Some kids continue to resist treatment regardless of what their parent(s) say. If your child continues to resist, remember this: *No matter how much they beg and plead, you must stay strong and reiterate that attending treatment is not a choice.* Be prepared for your child in her state of opposition to try to convince you that (1) there is no problem, (2) you caused the problem and if you force her into treatment you will make it worse, (3) you are the only one with a problem so why don't you go to therapy instead, (4) she can fix the problem on her own so don't waste your money on someone she doesn't even want to see in the first place, (5) if you make her go to treatment she will only sit there and won't talk, so it will be a waste of time and money, and (6) if you make her go to treatment, she will run away, self-injure more, or even worse, try to kill herself.

In the event that you are confronted with some of these statements, I thought it would be helpful to talk about each of them separately and provide ideas as to how to respond.

1. THERE IS NO PROBLEM!

Suggested response: "If that is true, then I will be so relieved. In fact, I really hope that there isn't anything to worry about. I love you so much and I don't want anything to happen to you. However, I am not an expert on self-injury and I can't make that determination. If you had signs and symptoms of cancer, I would not try to decide for myself whether you actually had this illness. Instead, I would take you to an oncologist, who specializes in cancer, and wait for their determination." This often drives the point home to your child that she has a very serious problem that needs immediate attention.

2. YOU CAUSED THE PROBLEM AND IF YOU FORCE ME INTO TREATMENT YOU WILL MAKE IT WORSE!

This statement almost always makes parents feel defensive. Unfortunately, becoming defensive does not help the situation. It is important to acknowledge your child's feelings. You may completely disagree with what she is saying, but remember it is how *she isfeeling* and *she is sharing* these feelings with you. The worst thing to do is to dismiss her feelings and/or to tell her that her perception of the problem is wrong. People have different perceptions. A trained practitioner will address this in treatment. For now, your daughter is willing to open up to you, so do not shut her down. If you do, she will most likely not share her feelings openly and honestly with you again. The suggested response below acknowledges her feelings:

"I am so sorry if you believe that I am the cause of the problem. I am sure there have been things that I have done that have led you to feel this way. It was never my intent to do anything to hurt you or to trigger your problems with self-injury. I am glad that you told me that you feel this way. I am convinced now, more than ever, that we need to set up some therapeutic appointments. Maybe we need to go to the first therapy session together so we can talk more about this. Perhaps we can also find a family therapist to help us because I certainly do not want to keep doing things that contribute to your scratching/cutting/burning."

By stating that you are willing to attend sessions with her and set up family therapy appointments, you are showing her that she will not have to enter treatment and recovery alone. In other words, you are declaring that you are "in it together" as a family. This type of statement is very powerful for kids. Many of them talk about this later in treatment and say that it was one of the driving forces that helped them work to get better.

3. YOU ARE THE ONE WITH THE PROBLEM, SO WHY DON'T YOU GO TO THERAPY INSTEAD!

I have found that the best way to respond to this is very similar to the last response listed ("You caused the problem and if you force me into treatment you will make it worse!"). It is important to remain neutral and to try not to become defensive. In part, your child may be saying this to make you angry. She may also be trying to deflect the focus off of her and place it on you. Parents often fall for this tactic. In the heat of the moment, an argument often erupts, with the parents responding angrily, "I am not the one who cuts herself, I am not the one who is scarring her body for life, I am not the one who is destroying the family, etc."

Not only are these statements not helpful, they are counterproductive and psychologically detrimental. Your child will walk away feeling even worse about herself. Instead of falling for this tactic and getting angry, validate your child's feelings. Make a statement that you are willing to attend therapy sessions with her to help resolve the problem.

4. I CAN FIX THE PROBLEM ON MY OWN, SO DON'T WASTE YOUR MONEY ON SOMEONE I DON'T WANT TO SEE IN THE FIRST PLACE!

Suggested response: "I am glad that you feel strong enough to overcome this problem on your own. I know that if you put your mind to it and work really hard you will overcome this problem. However, I am not sure if you can do it alone and that has nothing to do with you. This is a serious problem that needs to be treated aggressively. I have learned that it is very difficult to overcome self-injurious behavior without the support of a therapist and your family. To tell you the truth, I don't even know if I would want you to try to do it on your own. I love you and I want to learn how I can help you. I want to find an expert that has worked with individuals and families and can tell us what we can do to support you through treatment and recovery."

When addressing the issue of money, each family has different financial circumstances and will need to make decisions accordingly. There are wonderful experts that may be in-network with insurance companies so that therapy sessions involve only a co-pay. There are also wonderful experts in private practice who are often out-of-network providers. Families must work with their insurance companies to determine reimbursement, and decide what treatment options are feasible. Some families do not want to go through their insurance companies at all. In this case, the full fee of the practitioner would be out-of-pocket. In any case, the best way to try to respond to the money issue is to say that you will find an option that works for your family so that your child can get the help that she needs.

**5. IF YOU MAKE ME GO TO TREATMENT, I WILL SIT THERE
AND WON'T TALK, SO IT'S A WASTE OF YOUR TIME AND
MONEY!**

I cannot begin to tell you how many kids say this to
their parents, causing the parents to call me in a panic
believing that therapy will now be useless.   I assure
parents that although kids often say this, it is usually not
the case. In fact, most kids have a very hard time sitting in
complete silence. It feels awkward for them. Isn't this
true for most people? It is exceptionally rare to have even
an extremely resistant child come to my office and not
speak at all. In part, this is due to the fact that most therapists are trained to help kids feel comfortable so that they
are able to open up. Therefore, I have found that one of
the best ways to respond to this statement is to say something like this:

"I really hope that you are able to talk to the person
that you choose to work with. I know it is not always easy
to talk openly about a problem you are facing, but you
are strong. I believe that if you do find a way to open up,
you will be tremendously successful. It takes a lot of
courage to go to counseling and I believe that working
on oneself and overcoming a problem is never a waste of
time or money."

The first sentence reinforces the fact that your child has
a choice in who she sees. It also insinuates that she will be
attending therapy no matter what.   The rest of the
response provides your child with support and positive
reinforcement to get the help she needs. The last sentence
addresses "the waste of time and money," comment by

placing value on the therapy, which is important for her to hear from her parents.

There are a lot of parents who do not believe in therapy. You may be one of them. Kids are very aware when a parent looks down upon treatment. In fact, often continued resistance from a child to be in therapy comes from the modeling of a parent. They are quick to tell their therapist that their parent thinks "all psychologists are quacks." Everyone has a right to their opinion, just be mindful that if you have this opinion, your child is likely to adopt it as well, and not engage in the therapy that she needs to help her overcome her problem.

6. IF YOU MAKE ME GO TO TREATMENT, I WILL RUN AWAY OR EVEN WORSE I WILL TRY TO KILL MYSELF!

This is probably a parent's worst nightmare. You may find it hard to believe that your child would say something like this, however, it is actually a very common statement made in desperation by kids faced with treatment. I have found that one of the best responses to this type of statement is this:

"I love you and could never imagine life without you. This must be so scary for you to say something like that. To even think about hurting yourself or taking your life tells me how scary this must be for you. I know you don't want to be in therapy, but it is incredibly important for us to get you some help."

You can then use several of the other statements listed previously. You can talk about it being neglectful to not get her into treatment. You can make the analogy to cancer or drug abuse. You can offer to attend some sessions with her. You can let her know that she will have the ability to choose the right therapist for her. All of these things are incredibly helpful.

What is not helpful is backing down in response to her threat, and avoiding treatment. However, I am not implying that you should ignore her statement of harm and/or potential suicide. In fact, parents should take this very seriously. You may want to watch her 24/7 until you have confirmation from her therapist that she is not suicidal and can be safely left alone.

If she continues to make threats of harm or suicide and you do not feel like you can keep her safe, you may want to bring her to the closest emergency room where psychiatric personnel will evaluate her for safety. As discussed earlier, if it is determined that she is a danger to herself, she may be hospitalized and placed on a 72-hour hold. The hospital will most likely transfer her to an adolescent psychiatric unit where she will be monitored by medical and mental health practitioners until they determine that she is no longer at risk and can return home.

I wish that dealing with these convincing arguments to avoid treatment was all that parents were up against. Unfortunately, once parents have overcome this hurdle they are often faced with another one. Parents often ask me on the day of the initial appointment, "How do I get my child to come in to see you?" or "What do I say to her, because she is refusing to go?" Some parents will say "I cannot drag her into the car and make her come, can I?"

Obviously, this indicates that the child with the problem is very powerful in the family. I encourage parents to be firm and loving and not to take no for an answer. Below I have listed some things that I often guide parents to say to their child when in this type of situation.

* Remember that you have a choice in who you see. If you do not like this person, then we will interview some other therapists. Please give it a try.

* If you are unable to attend outpatient therapy because you are refusing to go to appointment, then we will have to start looking at either a day treatment program or a residential program where therapy is built into the program.

* Let's just get in the car and drive over there. If you still refuse, then you refuse. Once you are at the office, you can ask the therapist to come out to the car for the initial appointment. This is something most therapists will do.

* I will go with you to the first meeting if you would like. I am here to support you even though you don't want to go.

* If you don't go to the appointment, then you will not be able to go over to your friend's house tonight, the concert on Friday, your voice lessons, etc.

WHY DO INDIVIDUALS AVOID THE PROBLEM?

It is not uncommon for an individual to be in a therapy for a long period of time before feeling comfortable and safe enough to admit that they have a problem with self-harm. Skye, for example, who sought therapy for an eating

disorder, was in therapy for over one year with the same
therapist before she felt ready to discuss her self-injurious
behavior.   She recalls, "I just didn't want to admit to
having another problem in my life. I didn't want the attention for it, especially not for cutting. Nobody understands
it. They think people who cut are 'crazy' or 'psycho'.
Even though it is hard to have everyone always focusing
on my food, at least I am not ostracized for having an
eating disorder."

1. EMOTIONAL REASONS

As you have already learned, many individuals hide
their self-injurious behavior from others including their
therapists out of embarrassment, shame, or guilt. Obviously, a therapist who is unaware of the problem of self-
injury cannot treat it.   However, even when the therapist
is aware and the individual is open about her behavior,
treatment may be difficult. The individual may avoid
focusing on the problem because of discomfort (as in
Skye's case), an unwillingness to get well, or a resistance to
giving up a "trusted and beloved coping strategy."
Unfortunately, individuals for whom this last reason
applies are frequently opposed to any type of treatment
that will interfere with their deliberate, repetitive, self-
mutilating behavior. As a result, treatment of self-harm is
non-existent in their counseling sessions.

2. SOCIETAL VIEW OF THE PROBLEM

Another reason that people may avoid focusing on self-
injury in their counseling sessions involves societal views
of the problem. Society views individuals who self-injure

as "crazy" or at best "emotionally unstable." Words such as "shocking," "gruesome," and "horrific" exemplify the way people in our culture speak about this behavior. People avoid talking about it and do not want to be around someone who experiences this problem. While there has been some increase in acceptance in recent times, a common aversion to pain and injury still keeps many people away.

In the past, people who self-injured baffled the medical and mental health communities. They were viewed as a population that was untreatable. Even today, many mental health practitioners find it difficult to contemplate working with someone who self-inflicts bodily harm.

3. FEAR OF BEING LABELED

One way that society has chosen to deal with this problem is by labeling it and by labeling the people who engage in it. It is common for self-injury to be referred to as "cutting" and individuals who engage in it as "cutters." You have probably noticed by now that I do not refer to individuals who self-injure as "cutters." I have a very specific reason for not doing this and one that should be considered by all my readers.

I believe that is common practice in our society to label other people. This is particularly true when the person who is placing that label on someone else feels uncomfortable with that person's actions. Think about it. What purpose does labeling serve? Placing a label on someone creates an immediate distance between the two people; the labeler and the person being labeled. This in turn lowers

the discomfort being experienced by the labeler. In other
words, labeling someone is a way of saying this is who you
are (i.e. "a cutter") and I am nothing like you. And since I
am nothing like you (at least on the surface of things), I
can spend time with you in a less uncomfortable way.

INDIVIDUAL PERSPECTIVES ON ENTERING TREATMENT

The individuals whose stories are presented in this
book share a common thread. They all engage in some
form of self-injurious behavior. They deliberately, repeti-
tively, and often impulsively harm themselves as a way to
manage distressing emotions in their life. Their methods
may vary and the severity of their problems range, but
their coping mechanism is the same.

However, although they all engage in self-injurious
behavior, they will not all enter therapy in the same way.
Individuals enter therapy for different reasons. Their
thoughts about therapy, their perception of the presenting
problem, and their willingness and/or desire to change are
all different and unique.

For example, Cathy entered therapy at 15 years old.
She began self-mutilating following a sexual assault. She
was raped while on vacation with her family in the Caribbean. She was highly resistant to discussing the details of
her rape, but comfortable discussing her self-injurious
behavior. Cyndy is 16 ½. She began self-mutilating in the
8th grade. She has been able to keep her self-injurious
behavior a secret for many years. Recently her parents
found out about the problem and referred her for therapy.
Unlike Cathy, she is not comfortable discussing her self-

injurious behavior with anyone, including her new therapist.

Skye is 13 years old. She has been struggling with severe anorexia for several years. Her focus in therapy has always been on her eating disorder. In fact, she denied any other problem areas in her life up until recently. After one year of therapy, she admitted to sporadically self-injuring throughout the better part of her childhood. Alison is 15 years old. She is also suffering from an eating disorder. She was referred for treatment in a state of crisis by a colleague who was going on maternity leave. Alison recently reported her older step-brother to the police for molesting her. He is currently in jail. She is suffering from severe depression and has been having suicidal thoughts. In her initial interview she admitted that she has also been self-mutilating. Unlike Skye, Alison would like her self-injurious behavior to be the current focus of her treatment and is not interested in focusing on her other problems.

Lauren is 27 years old. She was referred for counseling by her psychiatrist. She has struggled on and off for many years with self-injury. Her self-injurious behavior is often impulsive and dissociative. In other words, she often does not remember the act of self-injury, but has wounds and witnesses to prove it occurred. She is extremely hopeful and highly motivated to work on her problems and to change her behaviors.

Brenda is the opposite. She is a 17-year-old female who came to therapy with low motivation and hope. She was referred for counseling after a fallout with her previous therapist due to a breach in confidentiality. She has struggled on and off for many years with self-harming behaviors including self-injury, eating disorders, promiscuity, and substance abuse. She has worked with many therapists in the past and has been asked to follow a variety of different treatment plans. Since nothing ever seems to work, she is not sure if she should even try.

Those who self-injure are desperately trying to give voice to pain that has no words. As you can see from the examples above, the origin of this pain is different for each individual. While specific interventions will vary for each individual, there are some key elements of a treatment plan that should be in place from the beginning in order to maximize the likelihood of a successful recovery.

CHOOSING THE RIGHT THERAPIST

The therapist's role is to work on the psychological components of the problem and help the patient move toward recovery. Psychotherapy is considered to be a crucial component of the treatment plan. As we have discussed on multiple occasions, there are many reasons why individuals self-injure. During the course of therapy, these reasons are explored with the person who is suffering. Understanding what triggers the person to self-harm is incredibly important for successful recovery. This exploration helps the child understand why she is engaging in the behavior. In order to accomplish this, the therapist will adjust to the person's level of insight, maturity, and development.

The therapist working with your child should cover the following important practices during the course of treatment.

❋ Set up a treatment participation agreement. This is a collaborative process. Decisions should be made together. The agreement can be written (formal) or verbal (informal).

❋ Create mutually agreed-upon goals. Goals should be objective and attainable.

❋ Include a written contract. The goal here is not only to avoid the self-injurious behavior, but also to increase the window of opportunity between the time the patient feels the urge to self-injure and the actual act. When an agreement is put into writing and signed by both the therapist and the patient, the patient often feels more obligated to follow through with their formal commitment.

❋ Have a medical practitioner assess the need for medical intervention. Remember safety comes first. It should be made clear to the patient that the therapist is not a medical doctor (unless they are) and therefore, she/ he will not examine the patient's injuries. If there is a medical concern due to injuries (i.e., need for stitches, splints, casts, etc.) then a referral to a medical practitioner (i.e., a doctor, physician's assistant, nurse, etc.) should be made.

❋ Provide a confidential, non-judgmental environment for your child to discuss her self-injurious behavior. Ideally she will feel free to discuss all aspects of her life and how they connect to her self-injurious behavior.

BUILDING A THERAPEUTIC ALLIANCE

Finding the right therapist is extremely important. This is particularly true for the resistant individual, who may enter treatment feeling guilt, fear and distrust toward both the therapist and the treatment. Accordingly, it is imperative to choose a therapist who can overcome these obstacles and create an environment of safety, comfort and support. Finding the right therapist is not always easy. However, it is a critical first step that will optimize the likelihood of successful treatment.

I strongly believe that therapy is only as successful as the "Goodness of Fit," between the therapist and the patient. In order for the therapeutic work to be successful, the therapist must build an alliance with the patient. If the level of comfort and trust necessary to build this alliance is not present, help your child find a different therapist. Changing therapists does not represent a failure on the therapist's part or the child's part. It simply means there may not be a good fit between them. Research has proven that the single most important factor in successful treatment is having a strong therapeutic alliance. In numerous studies, this was ranked above type of therapy (theoretical approach), and counselor training/experience.

It is very important for the therapist to be patient and non-critical with your child. Following your child's lead is also imperative, because it will reinforce to your child that she is in charge of her treatment. The moment the therapist takes a confrontational stance or leads your child in a direction she is not willing or ready to go, she will feel the therapist is attempting to control her and will either resist treatment or terminate all together.

Self-injury is confusing to many, including therapists that have not been trained in this area of psychology. There are usually few courses that a therapist can take to learn more about this issue, and it is often not even mentioned in textbooks. Accordingly, therapists interested in learning about self-injurious behavior have to seek out their own training from either a supervisor, consultant, or professor with expertise in this area. Due to this fact, it is not that easy to find a highly skilled practitioner with this area of expertise.

Although goodness of fit is incredibly important, parents should also inquire about the level of experience and training the therapist has in the area of self-injury. Parents may also want to inquire about the therapist's willingness to receive additional supervision or training in this area if they are going to work with their child. A good rule of thumb is to ask how many individuals the therapist has treated with the same problem. If the therapist says somewhere between one and five, then they have some understanding of the problem. If the therapist says between six and 15, then they have a good sense of what it takes to work with your child. If the therapist says between 16 and 30, they are very knowledgeable. Anything above 30 most likely means they have high expertise. Once you have found an expert to work with your child, she will be ready to start treatment and begin her journey towards recovery.

7

INTERVENTION AND RECOVERY

"It is not the mountain we conquer but ourselves."
- Sir Edmund Hillary

This chapter focuses on treatment intervention and recovery. It is my hope that after reading this chapter, caregivers will be more knowlegeable about what is helpful and what may be detrimental in the treatment of their child. In addition, they should feel better equipped to actively participate in the recovery process. As we have already learned, this problem is often associated with a roller coaster of emotions for both the family and the individual, from misplaced blame, to misunderstanding of intent, to simply not knowing how to help. Because of the stress that self-injury places on caregivers, it is often a great relief when the calls have been made, interviews are complete, and the child is finally receiving the help that she needs. Remember, with the right support, a person can recover fully from self-injurious behavior.

THE ROAD TO RECOVERY

It is not easy to recover from self-injury. As discussed earlier, self-injury is a complex problem that is often misunderstood by others as well as by the person affected. Therefore, treatment must include specific interventions that help the person identify the reasons for the behavior and eventually stop engaging in it, despite its addictive qualities.

Our society is changing. Our kids are more stressed out than ever before, burdened by high academic standards, extracurricular achievements, family financial concerns, and specific expectations as to how one must look in order to be popular and successful. In the past, these were issues that predominantly concerned adults. However, today our youth have taken on these pressures in a way that does not often serve them positively.

To relieve their anxiety, teens seek external outlets. Self-injury is one of those outlets, and the person who chooses it anticipates feeling less overwhelmed with each cut or burn. However, anyone who has ever struggled with self-injury knows that this behavior never really allows a person to "feel good" in the end. In fact, it is usually the opposite. The person often feels ugly and unworthy, which leads to a stronger desire to self-injure. Unfortunately, the more the person self-injures, the more she will feel the need to repeat, and escalate, the behavior. This leaves the person feeling defeated and helpless to either change the behavior or come up with alternatives. With frightening speed, what started out as a simple scratch becomes a debilitating problem.

In the beginning, since teens are generally not "breaking skin," they do not believe that they are doing any real harm, and thus do not see why they should enter treatment. When they graduate to cutting or burning, they justify the behavior by telling themselves that it is not hurting anyone else, and that it is their body to do with what they want. In addition, they recall how much better the behavior makes them feel. However, without treatment, the cycle of self-injury typically intensifies and becomes much more dangerous.

One of the main reasons that self-injury is considered difficult to treat is the uncertainty about the underlying cause or causes. Accordingly, in order to set up a proper treatment plan, all potential causes must be explored. In addition, the question of whether the person sees the problem as ego-syntonic or ego-dystonic should be addressed. When a problem is seen as ego-syntonic, it means that the person suffering from the problem does not think there is anything wrong with what she is doing and therefore, does not want any help. Patients with eating disorders often view their illness as ego-syntonic.

Psychological disorders that are ego-dystonic, such as depression and/or anxiety, are problems that the person very much wants to resolve. The person views these disorders as unpleasant, uncomfortable, and often distressing. Accordingly, their motivation to enter treatment is high.

Self-injury is tricky.   Some individuals see their
problem as ego-syntonic and some see it as ego-dystonic.
The good news is that even though individuals are often
initially resistant to enter treatment and give up a coping
mechanism that they believe works for them (ego-syntonic), upon working with a therapist, they learn to see
their behavior as dysfunctional and unhealthy (ego-dystonic).   This realization can provide the motivation to
stop the behavior and remain in recovery.

Often when the person initially views the problem as
ego-dystonic, their low motivation reflects the fact that
treatment for self-injury is complicated and filled with
relapses.   In addition, professionals vary in their opinions
about the best psychological treatment approach,
modality, and setting for the the person struggling with
self-injury, which can lead to frustration and confusion. It
takes a lot of courage to embark on a journey of recovery
from self-injury.   The good news is that there are wonderful treatments available with specialists who can help in
the recovery process.

SELF-INJURY IS A BEHAVIOR, NOT AN IDENTITY

I recognize that calling individuals who self-injure, "cutters" is a common practice.   However, I am adamantly
opposed to it because "cutting" is a behavior, not a
person.   Referring to a person as a "cutter" implies
that this is her identity. This could not be further from the
truth and is dangerous to even suggest.   First, the implica-
tion makes self-injurious behavior harder to give up
because it is not viewed solely as a behavior, but instead as

a whole person. In other words, if that is all that the person is, "a cutter," how would that person be able to give it up?

Imagine that someone approaches you, states, "You are a parent," and then says, "Stop being a parent." How would that make you feel? You would probably experience a variety of emotions, most likely including anger, confusion, and frustration with the person's request. Why? Because it would be difficult for you to change who you are. After all, you are indeed a parent, at least in part.

Now imagine someone approaches you and says, "You are a parent who yells at your children too much," and then says, "Stop yelling at your children." Your reaction to this would probably be very different. The person is telling you to change a behavior, not to change who you are. You might resent being told what to do or you might disagree that this is a problem; however, if you chose to make the change, it would be easier than in the former example because you would be changing a specific behavior and not your identity.

Second, I have found that when individuals identify themselves as "cutters," helping them to give up this behavior is twice as difficult for the reasons mentioned above. In this scenario, I must constantly remind my patients that they are not their behavior. I explain that they may be many things; a student, a friend, a son, a daughter, a colleague, an athlete, an artist, a philosopher, etc., but they are not self-injury. This is an action, not a personality trait or a role they fulfill in their life. Self-injury is something they choose to engage in, it is not who they are.

Third, if an individual has built an identity around self-injurious behavior, they are often much more frightened about what life would be like without it. It is not uncommon for people to avoid treatment out of fear that if self-injury is no longer a part of their life, they will become "an unknown person without direction or worth." Therefore, a large part of treatment for these individuals is to help them identify the other parts of themselves. In these circumstances it would be appropriate to ask the question, "Who are you if you are not someone who self-injures?"

TREATMENT OPTIONS

There are three main treatment options for self-injurious behavior; outpatient therapy, partial hospitalization (usually 6 to 12 hours per day; one to five days per week), and inpatient treatment. The most effective treatment for self-injury is usually a combination of cognitive behavioral therapy, insight-oriented therapy, interpersonal therapy, and medication.

Cognitive behavioral therapy helps identify the irrational, negative, and potentially destructive thoughts, feelings and behaviors that are present in the person's daily life. *Insight-oriented therapy* helps the individual gain insight into the underlying issues that lead to self-harm. *Interpersonal therapy* helps the individual initiate and maintain healthier and more positive relationships with others. *Medication* is used to treat any underlying psychiatric illness.

Because self-harm is often considered a symptom, it is not, in and of itself, usually treated with medication. However, it is not uncommon for individuals who self-mutilate to be diagnosed with an underlying psychiatric illness such as bipolar disorder (manic-depression), major depression, or anxiety. If this is the case, self-harm is considered one of the symptoms of that illness, which is often successfully treated with a combination of medication and talk therapy. Stabilizing the individual's mood and decreasing their urges helps to reduce the incidence of self-harm.

Once a treatment option is established, a treatment modality is selected to achieve the best outcome. There are several modalities available to treat self-injurious behavior. These include individual therapy, group therapy, and family therapy. It is not uncommon for individuals to utilize a combination of these different modalities. Typically, the determination is made by a mental health professional following an initial assessment. For the majority of patients, individual therapy is most highly recommended, with adjunct in-group and/or family counseling. As mentioned above, when outpatient therapy is not sufficient and the patient needs more intensive intervention, then inpatient treatment is often recommended. The next two chapters focus on these specific treatment interventions.

8

INDIVIDUAL THERAPY

"I longed for acceptance, my therapist welcomed me with open arms; I longed to be heard, she turned to listen; I felt worthless, she treasured me; I thought I was incapable, she gave me a chance to prove what I could do; I believed I was without talent, she called me gifted; I felt trapped in a shell, she set me free; I thought I could never do anything that mattered, she believed in me; I thought I was limp, she helped me to fly. And so I did, and I soared high."

- Cathy, age 15

There are a variety of different treatment interventions that are effective in supporting the individual who is self-injuring. There are also some treatment interventions that

are less helpful. However, before investigating the different treatment strategies and their records of success or
failure, I would like to share my philosophy on the
behavior itself.

I place a great deal of emphasis on treating patients
with respect, validation, and empathy. I believe it is
important to start where the patient is, and to move forward at their pace without hidden agendas. I do not
believe in placing the self-injurer in the role of the victim.
Instead, I work with the self-injurer to help them take full
responsibility for their recovery as well as for their acts of
self-harm and associated consequences. I recognize that
the person who self-injures often perceives their behavior
to be addictive. While I agree that self-injury can
become habit-forming, I see it as a behavior that is chosen
by the individual and therefore, one that can be avoided
and eventually stopped altogether.

It is important for parents to be aware that therapists
will differ in their approach to self-injury. I will describe
my approach here, however, I am not implying that it is
better than others. I frequently utilize two general types of
interventions, implemented together to help the individual to achieve greater success in recovery. Both stem
from the cognitive behavioral therapy described earlier in
this chapter.

The two types of interventions I combine are surface-
level interventions and deeper-level interventions. Con-
trary to what one might think, surface-level interventions
are not superficial. They are just as important as deeper-
level interventions; they simply stay at the surface of

things. These interventions are usually a good place to start with a patient because they provide the person with concrete, useful strategies to avoid self-harm.

Surface-level interventions provide the individual with tools that she can use to forestall future self-injurious behavior. These interventions are either at the behavioral level (see section on alternative behaviors) or focused on surface cognitions. For example, Alison self-injured to manage the distressing feelings she had in regard to sending her step-brother to jail. Her surface-level thought was "I got him in trouble." This thought triggered feelings of guilt, which in turn led to self-harm. Her surface-level thought was not superficial. It was an important thought and needed to be validated as it caused her great pain. However, it was a thought that was on the surface of things.

Once surface-level thoughts are identified, deeper-level thoughts can be explored. This process requires asking specific questions about the person's belief systems. For example, when I asked Alison what meaning or belief she connected to getting her brother in trouble (surface-level thought), she responded "being a bad person."

I explained to Alison that many people in her situation would have reported sexual abuse to the authorities just as she had, but would not have felt bad about doing so. Alison's distress about getting her brother in trouble came from the belief system that she held in connection to the thoughts. Moreover, the feeling of "being a bad person" caused her so much anguish that she regularly self-inflicted bodily harm.

I decided to move from surface-level interventions to deeper-level interventions with Alison.   Upon further exploration, Alison explained that "getting my step-brother in trouble" meant "having the rest of my family angry at me." Continuing on, Alison was able to recognize that having the rest of her family angry with her meant being "ostracized and criticized." Being "ostracized and criticized" meant being "a disappointment." Being "a disappointment" meant being "not good enough." Being "not good enough" meant being "worthless."

During this process, Alison was able to get to what I call an *emotional truth*.   Her feelings of worthlessness and "inner badness" were her deeper-level thoughts and the ones that truly triggered her self-injurious behavior. This type of intervention identifies the core trigger for the individual who chooses to engage in self-injury. Since these triggers are at the root of her negative thinking, they will likely affect her in all situations. For example, for Alison, reporting her step-brother to the police ultimately generated thoughts of worthlessness. However, these thoughts may be occur just as easily in another situation in which she feels like a disappointment or "not good enough."

Deeper-level interventions are always at the cognitive level. They are never behavioral. They are the thoughts that are present at the core of our being. The deepest-level thought is often the individual's greatest source of distress and the trigger which leads to self-injurious behavior. Identifying these deep thoughts is imperative for successful treatment. Without this identification, interventions and treatment remain on the surface of things and the risk of relapse becomes much greater.

THE COGNITIVE BEHAVIORAL CYCLE

Regardless of the specific underlying issues that lead to a person using self-injury as a coping mechanism, the treatment approach most often utilized is cognitive behavioral therapy. Cognitive behavioral therapy, also known as CBT, helps the individual identify the antecedent event that triggers self-harm by making the connection between thoughts, feelings, and behaviors. It is a treatment intervention often used when a person enters treatment and clearly presents a desire to refrain from self-harm. According to Slee et. al, (2008), patients who receive CBT have significantly greater reductions of self-harm and significantly greater improvements in self-esteem and problem solving ability than those who do not receive CBT.

Research shows that CBT alone has high success rates. Success rates are generally even higher with a combination of CBT and psychopharmacology (medication). Clinician observervations and research findings indicate that, when used in combination, various psychotropic medications and brief CBT consistently eliminate affective and psychiatric symptoms. Research also indicates that symptoms often return if either or both treatments are discontinued (Melfi et al., 1998; Parker et al., 2003).

When utilizing CBT, the individual is made aware that acts of self-injury are often triggered by event. An event is something that happens outside of the person. It can be good or bad. Initially, there should be no judgment placed on the event. It simply should be viewed as something that happens in the environment. An example of an event might be getting a good grade on a test, getting accepted into college or getting in an argument with a parent.

Once an event is identified, the individual explores how she connects that event to a feeling. For example, a person might say something like, "I am so happy because I got an A on my test," or "I am excited because I am going on vacation." We often do not realize that we directly connect events and feelings. In fact, we do it so frequently that many of us have come to blame events for the feelings that are elicited within us. This is interesting because in actuality it is not an event that causes a feeling, it is a thought about an event that causes a feeling.

For example, let's say two people experienced the same event; getting into Stanford University. The first person might say something like, "I am so excited because I received my acceptance letter to Stanford." This person's feeling is one of excitement and joy. One could easily make the assumption that the reason for the person's excitement and joy was the event; getting into Stanford. Remember, however, that it is not the event that causes a feeling; it is the thought about the event that causes a feeling. So what might this person be thinking? Probably that she wants to be a Stanford student. If her thoughts are that she interested in attending Stanford, then her feelings will be of excitement and joy. It makes perfect sense. But what if her thoughts were different? Would her feelings change? Let's take a look.

The second person also gets accepted into Stanford (i.e. the same event). However, upon hearing about his acceptance he declares, "I am so upset that I got into Stanford." Obviously, this person has very different feelings about his acceptance into the university. Why? His thoughts about the event are different. So what is he thinking? What if his thoughts are, "I don't want to go to Stanford. My parents want me to go to Stanford. I want to go to UC Berkeley." Clearly if he has no desire to go to Stanford he would not feel excitement or joy. He would feel the opposite, which is exactly what happened; he was upset.

Thoughts about an event do not only affect the way that the person feels, they also affect the way that the person responds. Therefore, the two people in the above example will behave differently due to their varying thoughts and feelings. The first person clearly wanted to go to Stanford (thought) and therefore was very excited (feeling) when she was accepted. Let's say that, in her excitement, she jumped up and down (behavior), told her friends and family (behavior) and could not wipe her smile off her face for the rest of the day (behavior). The second person clearly did not want to go to Stanford (thought) and therefore was unhappy (feeling) when he was accepted. Due to his unhappiness, he complained to his friends (behavior), isolated himself from his family (behavior) and sulked (behavior) for the rest of the day.

For both of these individuals, the cycle probably did not stop with these behaviors. More likely, their differing behaviors led to additional thoughts and feelings and then to additional behaviors. For example, for the first person, perhaps telling her friends about her acceptance led to thoughts about leaving them and losing their friendship, which in turn led to feelings of sadness. Perhaps she expressed this sadness by hugging her friends and telling them that she would miss them (behavior). For the second person, maybe his response of complaining to his friends led to his thoughts of how to explain to his parents that he did not want to go to Stanford, which in turn led to feelings of anxiety and ultimately to an avoidance of the subject when he got home (behavior).

Let's look at another example of how events trigger feelings and are often connected to emotions. The example will prove again that it is not the event that causes a feeling, it is the thought about an event that causes a feeling, which in turn leads to certain behaviors. Imagine that you have to work late one night. You are the last to leave your office and as you are waiting for your ride to pick you up after work (your car is in the shop), you see five huge men moving quickly towards you in the parking lot. The lot is dark and deserted and your ride is late. You do not recognize the men who are now almost at your side. What would you be feeling? Most likely you would feel afraid. You might even tell the person who finally arrives to pick you up, "I was so scared. While I was waiting for you five guys started moving in my direction really fast."

The five unknown men approaching you quickly in the deserted parking lot signify the event. The feeling that you experienced was fear. It would feel natural to explain to others that you felt a certain way because you were in a certain situation. However remember, it is not the event that caused you to feel fear, it was your thought about the event. So what were you thinking? Probably something like, "these guys are going to hurt me."

It makes sense that if your thoughts indicated you were in danger, you would experience worry, anxiety or fear. Think about how you would respond? Probably by trying to escape the situation in some way and finding safety. Let's say you decided to run away (behavior). As you are running (behavior) you would be having more thoughts about the event and your current behavior. For example, perhaps while you are sprinting across the parking lot you are wondering, "Are these guys following me?" Maybe this leads you to feel even more scared, which in turn leads you to run even faster (behavior). At this point maybe you wonder what you can do to escape danger (thought) and that you are frightened (feeling), so you reach for your cell phone and call 911 (behavior). The cycle of thoughts, feelings, and behaviors can be endless.

Now let's take the same event, but change the person who is experiencing it. Imagine that when five unknown large men approach this person in a dark deserted parking lot while she is waiting for her ride to pick her up after work, she feels relieved. Why? Her thoughts about the event must be different. So what is this person thinking? Well, what if she was thinking, "If someone were to attack me in this parking lot right now, these five huge men could protect me from harm." (I recognize that this is not the smartest thought an individual could have, but it is a good example and so I use it when illustrating the cognitive behavioral cycle).

If this person's thought is that these men can protect her from harm then her feeling would not be one of fear, but rather one of relief as she indicates. In turn, her behavior would also be different. She would not be likely to run away from the men, instead she would stay where she was or maybe even approach them and strike up a conversation (again not something I would ever encourage or advise). For her, the cycle probably also does not end here. As she approaches the men and begins to converse with them, she may have additional thoughts such as "these men are really nice" which leads to additional feelings of relief and happiness and then to additional behaviors (i.e. further conversation).

In both cases, the cognitive behavioral cycle completes itself several times before the interaction is over. Interestingly, it does not take hours or even minutes to cycle fully through, it takes seconds. We often do not realize how quickly we cycle through our thoughts, feelings, and behaviors in a given situation, with each step generating different reactions and responses.

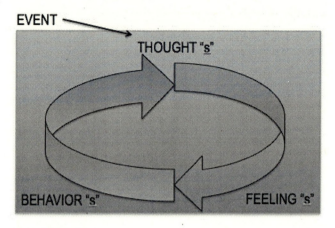

Cognitive Behavioral Cycle

Let's apply this cycle to self-injurious behavior. The behavior in the cycle is some form of self-harm (i.e. cutting, scratching or burning). During treatment, the therapist asks the individual to explore the cycle described above in reverse. In other words, the therapist asks the person to identify what they were feeling before they self-injured. With knowledge of the feeling(s) that led to self-injurious behavior comes the power to identify them as red flags and/or triggers.

Once a feeling is recognized, the therapist asks the individual to identify the thoughts that led to the feeling, as well as any event that may have triggered the thoughts. The reason for instructing the person to go backwards through this cycle is to help them identify the antecedents to their self-injurious behavior. Often individuals do not know why they engage in self-harm, they simply know that it makes them feel better. Exploration into this cycle can provide insight into the reasons for self-infliction. Without this awareness, treatment is often unsuccessful.

IMPULSE CONTROL LOG

The purpose of the impulse control log is to help individuals who self-injure begin to understand why they are inflicting self-harm. I truly believe that with awareness and knowledge comes the power to change. To help individuals become more aware, they are often asked to keep a daily log of their urges to self-injure. This is particularly helpful if they are not sure about the reasons behind their self-injurious behavior.

Similar to the backwards use of the cognitive behavioral cycle, the impulse control log can help the individual identify specific triggers that lead to the desire to self-harm. Most impulse control logs include the following categories: (1) date and time, (2) situation including location, (3) thoughts and urges, (4) feelings, (5) consequences of the behavior, (6) action taken, (7) outcome, and (8) insights.

Lauren loved using her impulse control log. She did not leave home without it. She took it everywhere with her and recorded every incident where she felt the urge to self-injure. Sometimes she acted on her urges, sometimes she did not, but in either case, it gave her insight into her behavior. She states, "It helped me recognize patterns in my behavior. There were very specific times that I would engage in self-harm. I had no idea that it was tied to incidents in which I felt out of control. This insight helped me to feel less vulnerable and more prepared for the onset of overwhelming feelings."

Cathy made a connection to her rape after several weeks of recording her urges to self-injure in her impulse control log. She recognized an interesting pattern in her behavior. She cut her shoulders with a knife every time she experienced incredible tension in her life. When experiencing other feelings, she cut elsewhere on her body.

To understand the significance of this pattern, some details of Cathy's rape need to be shared. Cathy's rapist not only sexually assaulted her, he physically abused her as well. As he held her hostage in his room, he used a belt to whip her and a knife to threaten her life. He strategically cut Cathy on her shoulders. The cuts were not deep enough to require stitches; they were not meant to be. They were meant to be reminders to her that he could have killed her if he wanted to. Cathy's self-inflicted wounds to her shoulders, made when stress levels become overwhelming for her, were directly correlated to the stress she had been under during her assault.

ALTERNATIVE BEHAVIORS

Most individuals who are motivated to stop self-injurious behavior enter treatment feeling lost as to how they will manage their emotions differently. Many anxiously request alternatives, hoping to find another "quick fix" to ameliorate their distress. The idea of delaying gratification is upsetting for them. Many of these people are so used to the instant relief brought on by cutting or burning that they cannot even fathom trying something new.

In my experience, providing individuals with concrete, usable solutions instills a sense of hope, which in turn can increase their motivation to continue in treatment. Many individuals who self-injure feel hopeless when they first enter treatment. They have made several attempts to stop the behavior and failed each time. The repeated failures make them feel increasingly "out of control" in their lives and helpless to change their situation.

Providing a person who self-injures with some basic tools they can use when they begin to feel the urge to self-harm is the first step in many treatment approaches. Since self-injury is an unhealthy coping mechanism, an exploration of healthy, alternative behaviors is vitally important. Increasing the person's variety of coping mechanisms can ultimately lead to a decrease in destructive behavior.

There are several steps necessary for success when using this intervention. First, it is important to figure out the reason why the person is self-injuring. For example, some individuals say, "I scratch to relieve tension," or "I burn to numb my feelings," or "I cut to feel alive." Second, it is important to validate to the individual that the self-injurious behavior is fulfilling a specific need for them. For example, a therapist might summarize, "You self-injure because it relieves tension and stress and makes you feel better."

Many people are afraid to provide validation to the person who self-harms. They become concerned if they validate the behavior, that the person will continue to engage in it. Remember that validation is not the same as encouragement and that you are not validating the act of self-injury as much as you are validating the reasons for the act. In other words, you are offering empathy and understanding, not permission to continue. Research shows that when the individual is feeling understood and validated, they are less likely to self-harm.

Nonetheless, if you are worried that you are sending the wrong message to the individual who is self-injuring, clarify your intentions. Tell her that you certainly do not want her to continue to self-harm, but that you understand why she is doing it. Maybe you can even help her find alternative ways to manage her stress. This brings me to the third step; exploring other behaviors that could potentially fulfill the same need as self-injury. For example, ask the question "What else could you do to relieve tension and stress and feel better?"

In order to successfully find alternative behaviors to self-injury, *the alternative behavior must fulfill the same need.* I cannot reinforce this enough. If the alternative behavior does not, then the therapist has missed the boat and the individual will not feel comforted or safe. In turn, she will likely revert to her self-destructive behaviors.

Imagine feeling stressed out at work. You are feeling anxious due to some conflicts with your co-workers. You are looking for a way to reduce the tension that is building inside of you. So you do what you have always done, you go to the gym and get in a long, hard workout. Afterwards, you feel better. But what if you were not really

stressed out and you were feeling sad instead. Perhaps
your feelings were hurt by some comments that were
made about you at a staff meeting. If you went to the gym
to work out thinking that you would be decreasing tension
and stress but afterward still felt sad and hurt, then the
behavior (going to the gym) did not fulfill your specific
need, which was to decrease sadness.

I often encourage my patients to make a list of at least
five alternative behaviors that fulfill specific needs or provide them with at least some form of temporary distrac-
tion. The behaviors must be safe and do not necessarily
have to include some form of physical action. In fact, I
encourage at least a few to be things that can be done any-
where and at any time. This is important so as not to limit
the use of the alternative behavior from the beginning.
For example, Lauren initially came up with six alternative
behaviors, all of which focused on some form of physical
activity. The problem was that, realistically, if she was sitting in a work meeting and tensions were rising, she would
not be able to sneak away and go to a kick-boxing class or
out for a run.

In addition, I ask patients to be thoughtful about the
different emotions they experience that lead to self-harm
and then to come up with behaviors that address each specific emotion such as anger, sadness, stress, boredom, etc.
This is important so that the person has numerous comforting activities from which to choose, depending on how
she is feeling at the time. The greater the variety of alternative behaviors that the person has on their list, the more

likely they are to find one that works for them in a specific situation.

For example, Nadia and Cathy loved to journal. Writing was a wonderful way for them to regularly comfort themselves in place of self-injury. Elaine liked physical exercise. Although she was not able to do it all of the time, she learned how to sit with her uncomfortable emotions until she was able to get to gym. Just sitting with your feelings and learning to tolerate your own distress can be extremely helpful. Challenging negative or irrational thoughts can serve a similar purpose. Therapists often encourage their patents to utilize these internal coping mechanisms during their individual session times.

Talking to a trusted friend is another alternative behavior. Nadia found this to be highly beneficial. She also began to knit. Needlepoint, painting, ceramics or any other type of arts and crafts project can be distracting and relaxing for the individual. Joey liked to listen to music and Brian liked to play his drums as alternatives to self-injury. Alison liked to sing and Skye liked to dance. Artistic expression can be powerful in the fight against self-injurious behavior.

It is important to realize that identifying alternative behaviors and then testing them out will be a process of trial and error. Some new behaviors may work and some may not. The goal is to give the individual options when feeling the urge to self-harm. It is also important to realize that, in the beginning, alternative behaviors may not provide the same "quick fix" relief that self-injury does. What these alternative behaviors provide is a way to experience

genuine emotion, which will ultimately help individuals
cope better in a positive way.

Symptom Jumping

I mentioned earlier that alternative behaviors must be
safe. I would like to expand on this notion. It is not
uncommon for individuals who self-harm to switch from
one self-injurious behavior to another. This can be seen
while the person is in recovery as an attempt to come up
with an alternative coping mechanism, or it can be seen in
pre-recovery while the person is in the midst of repetitive
self-harm.

Unfortunately, I have heard several accounts in which
either the patient or the therapist has come up with unsafe
alternative behaviors for the patient to utilize.

As mentioned previously, I have had patients tell me that a
previous therapist instructed them to snap a rubber band
on their wrist every time they had the urge to self-harm or
to put their hand in a bucket of ice water to achieve the
same pain or numbing effect they sought previously. The
problem with these alternative behaviors is that they are
still self-injurious and can be unsafe.

Lauren reports that she often did more damage by
snapping a rubber band on her wrist then she did when
cutting. She questions "Have you ever seen the welts that
you can give to yourself if you snap a rubber band hard
enough? It is not a pretty sight." Joey used to put a
rubber band around his neck. He said it was less noticeable there. He would actually entice others to snap it for
him. "I made a game out of it and never had to take

responsibility for my actions. If anyone ever asked me what happened to my neck, I could simply say my friend did it." Sara also did not have to take responsibility for her actions. She ended up in the emergency room with frost-bite on her fingers. When the doctor questioned how this could have happened in the middle of summer, she explained that her therapist had told her to stick her hand in a bucket of ice water as a way to help her "feel alive."

As mentioned before, the idea behind these suggested behaviors is that they represent less-dangerous forms of self-injurious behavior and therefore, are acceptable alternatives. Most often, well-meaning people (usually adults) make these recommendations in an attempt to help, not hurt. These people recognize that if an individual is motivated to self-injure, she will find a way to engage in that activity. Therefore, lessening the degree of self-injurious behavior is at least a step in the right direction. The problems with this line of thinking include: (1) these suggested behaviors are unsafe, (2) they prolong the use of self-injurious behavior as a coping mechanism, and (3) they send a strong message to the individual that self-harm is the only option to feel better.

THE PRESSURE COOKER THEORY

When encouraging alternative behaviors, it is important to consider "The Pressure Cooker Theory." This theory is based on the misbelief that people *have to get their feelings out or they will explode.* There is absolutely no evidence to support the pressure cooker theory. In fact, throughout history people have been known to be able to handle tremendous amounts of distressing emotion. The human mind has incredible capabilities that are often overlooked or minimized. Techniques that promote the expression of feeling, also known as *catharsis*, reinforce the inaccurate idea that the mind cannot withstand a high level of distressing emotion. In turn, this fallacy encourages the individual who so desperately desires relief to turn to a harmful physical or behavioral means to achieve it.

As mentioned earlier, many individuals who suffer from self-injurious behavior often come from families where the expression of emotion is either directly, or indirectly, discouraged. In Joey's home, for example, anger was always associated with an act of physical aggression. Accordingly, as an adolescent, he is fearful that if he allows himself to feel anger, physical aggression will follow. Knowing all too well the dire consequences that are associated with physical assault, he refrains from feeling anger at all. In fact, he tries to avoid feeling anything at all. He states, "I am successful in doing this most of the time, but when any feelings begin to emerge especially anger, I immediately numb myself to them by burning my skin."

Another problem with the pressure cooker theory is that strategies to help the individual get their feelings out may lead to an overstimulation that, in and of itself, can be distressing. This overstimulation can contribute to a greater sense of helplessness and may create even more "out of control" feelings.

Lauren was diagnosed with bipolar disorder following her first major incident with self-injurious behavior. She was in a manic phase and engaging in several self-destructive behaviors when she was instructed by her therapist to stimulate her body in more positive and healthy ways. She took this statement literally and spent the majority of her day engaging in some form of physical activity (i.e. long hours at the gym, running her dogs at the dog park, rearranging the furniture in her room, etc.). Afterwards, she reported that it was, "...like adding fuel to an already out of control fire." She ended up feeling more distraught then before and self-injured to a greater extent.

INSIGHT-ORIENTED THERAPY

One of the main goals in long-term individual therapy is to help the person articulate their thoughts and feelings so that they can begin to tolerate the distressing emotions that lead to their desire for self-harm. Once these emotions are better accepted, the individual can begin to explore the underlying issues that are present as they self-injure. Another goal is to begin to challenge their "all-or-nothing" thinking style, in which they view things in extremes or absolutes. This is an important part of treatment because the individual who is self-injuring typically either considers their emotions as "all-consuming" and destructive, or feels completely "void" and numb.

These goals can be achieved in treatment sessions through verbal exploration between patient and therapist, or through written assignment and review. I have found that journaling can be incredibly therapeutic for individuals who self-injure. Journaling can help the individual organize her thoughts and feelings, increase her insight into her problems, and help her reach conclusions about the reasons she self-injures. It is a safe, constructive activity that I often encourage as an alternative behavior.

Moreover, many individuals are resistant to "talk therapy." If this is the case, it can be helpful for the therapist to ask her patient if she would prefer journaling during her free time and then reviewing her entries during the next session. Naturally, the person would have to be comfortable sharing these entries and would not be forced to do so.

Conversely, if the individual is open to discussing her behavior, a verbal exploration of the topics listed below can serve as a model of self-expression, which is one of the main goals in treatment. Both talk therapy and journaling/review can help build a trusting therapeutic relationship, which is imperative for successful treatment. There are other ways to engage patients as well, including art therapy, music therapy, drama therapy, etc., all of which can help them accomplish the goals mentioned above. Most therapists are flexible in their approach because they recognize that the ultimate goal is finding a technique that will lead to successful recovery.

9

OTHER TREATMENT OPTIONS

"Individual therapy didn't work for me. Groups were better. I liked talking to other people who were going through the same thing as me. It made me feel less crazy and alone. Group wasn't enough though, so I ended up going to a residential program where I got the help I needed in a group setting, which worked really well for me."
- Collin, age 16

Individual therapy is not right for everyone. Although it is the treatment modality most common utilized by therapists who treat individuals with self-injurious behavior, other options are also available. This chapter focuses on alternative treatment options.

GROUP THERAPY

Group therapy is often used as a treatment modality for self-injurious behavior. Groups typically have eight to ten members and meet on a weekly basis for a predetermined amount of time (usually 60 to 90 minutes). Most therapists use group therapy as an adjunct to individual therapy and not as a substitute. This is primarily because the individual suffering from self-harm needs extensive, personalized attention to meet their specific needs in treatment and recovery.

Group therapy has significant benefits that other treatment modalities cannot provide. First, it provides a therapeutic setting in which the person does not feel so alone. When an individual is struggling with self-injury, she often feels like nobody in the world understands her. Joining a group and meeting other people experiencing similar struggles helps her feel less isolated. Second, it gives the individual an opportunity to express her thoughts and feelings verbally to others. Lack of verbal self-expression is common among self-injurers and is often a primary reason why that the person self-injures.

Third, it allows individuals to practice building their frustration tolerance. Since they share a therapy session with other people, they do not have full control of what is discussed. Topics raised by other group members could potentially frustrate them. Group then becomes a place where they can deal with their mounting distress and learn to cope with others who may cause it (usually unintentionally). Individual therapy gives the person more control over their session because they can choose the topics that they would like to discuss. It is possible that the individual becomes frustrated with her therapist during individual counseling as well, but the likelihood is decreased in this treatment modality.

As mentioned above, group therapy is often used as an adjunct to individual therapy for the self-injurer. However, there are circumstances in which group therapy is recommended as the primary treatment intervention. The reason for this is typically when the individual refuses to attend individual therapy sessions, but is willing to participate in group therapy sessions. As mentioned in previous chapters, it is important to start where your child is starting. Treatment may be mandatory, but the type of treatment is not. It is preferable for the individual to attend individual therapy in order to receive specialized treatment interventions. However, if the person refuses to go, participating in a group can be a way to begin the therapeutic process.

Another reason that group therapy may be recommended is for the added benefit of peer co-counseling. Often groups are structured so that individuals who have been through treatment and are currently in recovery can help other group members in the initial stages of the problem. This is often invaluable for the struggling self-injurer. Peer co-counselors can be particularly insightful and supportive in the group process, sharing specific intervention tools that they have learned during their own individual counseling. However, the group facilitator must also make sure that negative interaction between group members does not occur.

We know that our kids seek information and support
from their friends all the time. Unfortunately, they do not
always receive the type of support we would choose for
them. Often they are encouraged to maintain their
problem, not to engage in treatment and recovery. Some
peers do this intentionally and others do it unintentionally. The effects, however, can be similar. What would
happen if something like this happened during group
therapy?

Medical and mental health professionals agree that
when self-injury patients are in treatment groups or
recovery programs, they often join together and discuss
their signs and symptoms as a way to gain emotional support and validation for their struggles. Although this can
be a positive influence at times, it can also become a negative one if they use this contact to share tricks that will
help them continue their self-harm.

Most commonly, individuals struggling with self-
injury collectively try to minimize their symptoms and justify their problem. They defend their coping mechanism by claiming that it is "the only thing that works," and
convince themselves, that it is "not that big of a deal." I
have had several patients tell me that they justify their self-
injury as a way to numb their pain. They state that it is
their body and they have the right to do what they want to
it. In addition, they often see self-injury as part of their
identity. To take this away from them would involve not
only a loss of control but also a loss of self.

FAMILY THERAPY

Family therapy is indicated as a primary treatment intervention when a child is struggling with a serious problem that affects the entire family system. This is often the case when the individual is engaging in self-injurious behavior. As we have discussed throughout this book, it is common for parents, siblings, and/or extended family members (especially if they are living in the home) to be affected by this behavior.

As illustrated, the act of self-injury often results in fear, confusion, and dismay among family members. While reactions may vary, many of them are either unhelpful or, in extreme cases, psychologically detrimental, to the individual sufferer. When this is the case, family therapy can address the conflicts that develop among family members. If your family is feeling torn apart because self-injurious behavior is present in your home, family therapy can help you heal.

In general, family therapy provides a safe place for family members to learn better ways to interact with each other and resolve conflicts. It is often short-term, and may include all family members or only those who are most able to participate (this is called separated family therapy). The specific treatment plan will depend on the individual family.

Family therapy is often used as an adjunct to other types of mental health treatment. This is particularly true if a family member has a serious problem like self-injury. In cases like these, family therapy can help parents cope if their child is cutting, burning, scratching, and/or

punching herself. It can also improve strained relationships, and help parents support their child through treatment and recovery. The sufferer will need her own individualized treatment plan in addition to family therapy.
This plan may include weekly individual therapy, weekly
group therapy, and possible medication monitoring. If
this is not enough, the child may need inpatient care.

If the child ends up going to a residential treatment
center, the family is often able to attend family therapy
sessions while their child is there. Most programs have a
family therapy component. Sometimes a family engages
in therapy even if their child refuses to participate in their
own individualized treatment plan (whether it is outpatient or inpatient), just to gain knowledge and support.
Because family therapy allows the parents and other
family members to participate, it is often sought out by
parents.

Many parents ask me what they need to do to find a
good family therapist. It is not much different than what
you would do to find a good individual therapist (see
Chapter 6: Overcoming Resistance and Entering Treatment). You can ask your primary care doctor for a referral
to a family therapist. Another resource is to ask your
family and friends for recommendations based on their
own experiences with a family therapist. Your health
insurer, employee assistance program, clergy, or state or
local mental health agencies may also offer recommendations.

Remember it is important to find a therapist who will
be a good fit for your family. Before scheduling an

appointment, get a sense of the person on the phone. Will the therapist's approach, therapeutic style, and personality match those of your family members? If so, schedule an initial intake and test the waters. Remember you do not need to continue meeting with a therapist that does not seem to be a good fit for the family. This is trickier than when looking for a therapist for an individual because there are more people involved. Everyone in the family has to feel good about the person in whom they have chosen to confide.

In summary, family therapy can be an invaluable treatment modality that supports a family system that has a member engaging in self-injury. This is particularly true if the family does not understand the self-injurious behavior or how to best offer support to their loved one. Fear and misunderstanding often result in unintentional but profound family conflict. Family therapy can help pinpoint the specific concerns of each family member, improve communication, and aid in finding new ways to interact positively. Through hard work and commitment, families can achieve a sense of understanding and togetherness.

INPATIENT TREATMENT

Parents often ask me if their child would benefit from inpatient treatment. They are uncertain as to whether outpatient therapy will be enough and they want their child to get as much help as possible. The answer is not an easy one because every child is different. However, there are several factors that can help determine if an inpatient setting is appropriate for your child.

First, it is important to look at the level of risk associated with your child's self-injurious behavior. I find it helpful to think about this as a continuum based on the type of self-injury, the location of the self-injury, the object used, and the pace of escalation. For example, if your child is scratching herself with paper clips on her forearms, the level of risk is still moderate, and outpatient therapy is an appropriate place to start. However, if your child is cutting her wrists or neck with a razor blade, inpatient treatment may be necessary.

Inpatient treatment can take place in a hospital setting or in a residential treatment center. Hospitalization is considered one type of inpatient treatment. While self-injury can be treated without hospitalization, when there are high safety risks, the person may need to enter a hospital. A person would be hospitalized, for example, if she does not believe that she can stop the self-injurious behavior and is worried that she might unintentionally kill herself. This occurred with one of the patients mentioned earlier. Her self-injurious behavior escalated over the course of several weeks until one day she cut herself almost down to the bone. She admitted that she felt completely out of control and was not sure if she could keep herself safe. She was admitted to the hospital accordingly.

When an individual is ready to be discharged from the hospital, there is often a step-down program offered to her so that she does not go from a highly structured and safe environment to the complete opposite. These step-down programs are often called partial hospitalization programs (PHP's) or intensive outpatient programs (IOP's). They are almost always located at the hospital and function as a day treatment setting. The person usually attends the program for six to twelve hours per day. They may begin attending five days a week, and then taper down to two to three days per week until they are ready for discharge.

Residential treatment programs are another type of inpatient treatment. These programs provide a structured clinical environment where individuals receive intensive therapeutic support. Residential programs are typically run by a group of professionals who are highly trained in the problem area. People generally enter a residential facility when their self-injurious behavior has escalated to the point that they are not functioning in their daily lives. This may include being unable to attend school, activities or work, becoming isolated from friends and family, and ignoring responsibilities such as chores, homework, and even personal hygiene. Often an outpatient therapist will recommend a residential treatment program when individual therapy has not progressed. Unfortunately, residential treatment programs for self-injurious behavior are not easy to find.

Karen Conterio and Wendy Lader, Ph.D. co-founded a program called SAFE (Self Abuse Finally Ends) Alternatives in 1985. This program was the first structured inpatient program for deliberate self-harm. As internationally-acclaimed experts in the field, they have helped thousands of patients recover from this problem. SAFE Alternatives is a world-renowned treatment program that, in its more than twenty years of operation, has helped thousands of people successfully end self-injurious behavior. Other treatment facilities have sought to replicate the work begun by Conterio and Lader.

Most residential facilities have a treatment team of experts that provide therapy, education, and support to their patients. A primary goal is often to empower patients and help them to identify healthier ways to cope with their emotional distress. For example, the SAFE Alternatives philosophy and model of treatment focus on shifting control to the client, giving them to power to make healthy choices, including the choice not to self-injure. They strongly believe that "Quality of Life is a Choice."

As a way to support individuals who are struggling with self-harm, Conterio and Lader authored a wonderful book, which has been mentioned in earlier chapters. *Bodily Harm: A Breakthrough Healing Program for Self-Injurers*, offers a comprehensive treatment regimen for those who are suffering. If your child is struggling with this problem, I highly recommend that you get a copy of this book for her. It will educate her, help her to feel less alone, and provide her with specific tools for intervention and recovery.

10

ENDING TREATMENT AND RELAPSE PREVENTION

"When I decided to end treatment, I never thought I would go back to my old ways, but it happened several times. The key is to learn from your relapses and find ways to deal with similar situations differently the next time. Remember, you are not a failure for relapsing. Relapse is a part of recovery."
- Joey, age 17

When your child's therapist informs you that she is ready to stop treatment, it is important to inquire whether or not relapse prevention has been addressed in their sessions. It is not uncommon for a child to relapse. Unfortunately, patients can fall into old traps and revert back to negative behaviors. The trick is to help the child learn to identify these traps and make choices before they feel like they are in crisis and have the urge to self-injure. If the therapist is able to do this, the chances of relapse are greatly reduced. This is a very important part of treatment and, unfortunately, one that is often overlooked.

REASONS FOR RELAPSE

There are several possible reasons for relapse. One of the main reasons that people relapse is because of *secondary gains*. Secondary gains are indirect reasons for maintaining unhealthy behaviors such as self-injury. They are secondary to the primary reasons already discussed.

For example, think about a child who received a lot of attention from her family when she was engaging in self-injurious behaviors. Previously, she may not have received much attention at all. She was one of five children in the home, and both her parents worked full-time jobs in order to support the family. Nannies were inconsistent, her older siblings wanted nothing to do with her, and her younger siblings were a pain so she avoided them. Although her problem with self-injury did not develop because of a lack of attention, the increased attention is a secondary gain for her, and in turn, a reason for her to resist recovery.

Most kids are unaware of the presence of secondary gains. However, they are very powerful and can stop treatment progress and recovery. Once the therapist can help the child connect her fears to her resistance, it is much easier to work with her effectively. For example, once this girl understood that she was resisting treatment because she was afraid of losing her family's attention, she was able to discuss her fears openly and receive reassurance that her parents' support would not end. The family worked hard to be more present for one another, and to support her through typical adolescent issues as well as through her urges to self-harm.

Another common reason for relapse is *self-sabotage.* Self-sabotage is when the child puts herself in situation that will entice her to self-injure. For example, if she seeks out the company of others who also engage in self-injurious behavior, she places herself at much greater risk of engaging in these behaviors too. Although she is often aware that choosing to be with these people will place her in an extraordinarily difficult and stressful situation, she does it anyway. Most often, individuals do this because they are not quite ready to give up self-harm. In any case, it is a set-up for relapse and should be avoided until the person is far enough along in recovery to withstand the influences of others. The therapist and the patient can determine together when this time has arrived.

Another possible reason for relapse is a *fear of change.* Change is hard for many people. The child may be losing part of her identity when she says good-bye to her self-injurious behavior. Remember that individuals connect and identify with this coping mechanism. Because they see themselves as "cutters" and take this behavior on as their identity, they have a hard time letting it go. Separation is part of the therapeutic work and often very difficult. For many people, self-injury has been their best friend, their security blanket, and their safety net. When they are faced with giving it up, they worry that they will be lost and alone. Many things in a person's life change when they rid themselves of self-harmful behavior. It is common to revert back to what is comfortable and familiar when faced with change, even if it is not healthy, because it *feels* safe.

Another reason for relapse is *distrust in recovery.* Even though caregivers know that the loss of self-injurious behavior is for the better, the child may not fully believe this to be true. In the beginning of treatment, most individuals resist therapy because they believe that they will lose the only coping mechanism that works for them. Later in treatment, this distrust may or may not still be present. In either case, additional feelings of distrust may present themselves. The person is losing a coping mechanism that has served a purpose. Even with other coping mechanisms in place, she may not feel that these alternatives provide the same outlet for her needs.

Patients need to be reminded that recovery is a process. It does not happen overnight. If the child is used to a quick fix for her problems, when her needs are not met immediately she may revert back to old patterns because the new ones are "not working."

Lastly, having a low *deserve level* is another possible reason for relapse. The child may not believe that she deserves to get well. She may reject recovery due to low self-esteem and low self-confidence. Accordingly, building up her deserve level is particularly important in treatment. The goal is to help the child increase her overall sense of self-worth.

RELAPSE PREVENTION

Anticipation and preparation are the best strategies in relapse prevention. Do not be afraid to talk to your child about her triggers. If you know what the triggers are, you can help your child anticipate the events, thoughts, and feelings that may lead to self-injurious behaviors. Try to discuss ways that your child will be able to handle a potentially difficult scenario so that she is not caught unprepared. You might role play or model ways in which she could cope with her distress. Coming up with alternative coping mechanisms ahead of time will help your child feel more in control when dealing with potential struggles.

Initially, you may need to avoid triggers altogether. Although this may not be ideal, it may be imperative in order for your child to resist relapse. For example, you may need to re-think a planned Hawaiian vacation if seeing others in bathing suits with a tan and no scars on their body will trigger feelings of sadness, frustration, and unworthiness in your child. In addition, it can be very stressful for the self-injurer to try cover up their scars so no one will judge them. I cannot tell you how many times I have worked with families who have attempted a relaxing family vacation, but ended up coming home early because their child's mental stability was affected and their self-injurious behavior increased.

Changing your plans and your lifestyle can be frustrating. If you are feeling annoyed, go back to what was discussed earlier in the book. Think about how you would react if your child had a medical illness. If she was in the midst of chemotherapy treatments that interfered with your family going to Hawaii for the week, would you be angry with her? You might be disappointed, but probably not as irritated and frustrated as with her intentionally causing self-harm. Remind yourself that she did not ask for this problem and ultimately would prefer that things went back to the way they used to be. I doubt that she is happy with the fact that she will be missing out on a trop-ical vacation due to her self-injurious behavior.

ENDING TREATMENT

Termination of treatment should be carefully planned by the therapist. Typically, a therapist begins termination with a patient 4-6 weeks prior to their last appointment. This gives the therapist and patient enough time to dis-cuss the work they accomplished, relapse prevention, and any other important details to support a successful end to therapy.

It is often very helpful for parents to ask their child's therapist what their termination policy is. This is impor-tant in case their child has a relapse or develops some other problem for which they need support. There is often a need to re-enter counseling for a check-in. Most therapists have what is called an *open-door policy*, which means that they are willing to see the patient again if a need arises. As a parent, you do not want to discourage further appointments if your child is struggling. Usually these types of appointments help keep the person on track. They are not regular weekly sessions, but rather one or two appointments to guide and support the child intermittently.

It is not easy to overcome self-injury. Remember that you as parents can be a wonderful resource for your child. This is a difficult journey for the whole family. However, with your love, support, and guidance, your child has a much better chance of full recovery. In the next chapter, I would like to share with you some inspiring stories of treatment and recovery from the perspectives of different individuals and their family members.

11

Inspiring Stories

"The world breaks everyone, and afterward, some are strong at the broken places."
- Ernest Hemingway

I would like to share some personal stories written by individuals who have struggled with self-injurious behavior. It is my hope that these inspirational stories will not only help enhance your understanding of the problem, but also aid in your decision to get your child the help she needs in order to stop this devastating behavior. Remember, ultimately with proper understanding and support, your child can overcome the problem of self-injury.

Francesca, Age 19

When I first started cutting myself I was 14 years old and a freshman in high school. I started getting depressed

when I was 12 years old. My depression got worse and by
the time I was in high school it was really bad. I felt academic pressure from my classes, social pressure from
friends, and family pressure at home. I know some people
have a breaking point and then spontaneously cut, but for
me it was different. It happened almost by accident.

One day, I went to feed my cat and while I was opening
a can of cat food, the lid cut my hand. My reaction surprised me - I immediately felt calm. It was weird because
it was something I focused on completely, and that made
the stress around me just fall away. It was peaceful. I
couldn't stop thinking about how calm I felt. Later that
night I went to take a shower and decided to take a razor
blade to my arm. I didn't know how to get the blade out
of the razor so I just tried to cut myself from a million different directions until I found the right angle and made
myself bleed. I knew it would hurt, but I didn't care
because I knew it would make feel calm. I wanted to feel
calm. The pain from the cut only lasted a few minutes, but
the feeling of calm lasted longer.

After that first night, I began to cut regularly. After I
cut I felt guilty. I knew what I was doing was not normal
and was a way of hurting myself, which was not good. I
was worried that people would be disappointed in me. I
knew it would scare them and freak them out. I also knew
that if I continued to cut, people would probably start
looking at me differently.

What I was not fully prepared for was how hard I would
have to work to hide the cuts. I knew that if people found
out, I would be pressured to stop and I was not willing to

do this. Second, I knew there was no way to be close to people if they knew and were constantly worried about me. How could they feel comfortable with me if they worried every time they saw blood under my fingernails or knew that if they accidentally bumped into me, it would cause me pain because I had cuts all over my body that were not fully healed.

I often worried that blood would seep through my clothes and reveal my secret. I remember not wanting to change in gym class because I was petrified that someone might see my wounds and judge me for them. I had to hide everything all the time. I hid my cuts and I hid my razor blades. I hid my cuts by covering them up and by cutting in places that people would be less likely to notice. I hid razors in my clothes, in the soles of my shoes, in the back of my cell phone, and in a mint tin in my backpack. I took them wherever I went because I needed them to cope.

A lot of people ask me how long I self-harmed. The answer is that it went on for 4 ½ years. However, during that time, it was never consistent because on multiple occasions, I tried to stop. It was never easy. Sometimes I would be self-injury free for a week or a few months, but then the pressures became too great and I went back to what made me feel better. I think I knew at the time that I was not ready to give it up for good. It became really bad in my senior year. I gave up trying to quit and the cutting got worse than ever before. The pressures of college and negative relationships with peers caused me incredible distress. Many of my friends were depressed and some were feeling suicidal, which brought more worry and concern into my life. I graduated with my coping mechanism fully integrated into my life.

After graduation, I met someone who helped me quit. He made me feel important and loved. He helped me to see that I needed to learn to love myself. I knew that self-injury was a coping mechanism, not a way to truly take care of myself. I made a commitment to stop, but the problem was that it was more for him and for the relationship than for me. When you are quitting for someone else it is a good start, but not until you quit for yourself are you truly going to overcome the problem. I think the longest I went without cutting was six months.

Another common question that comes up a lot is how I feel about my scars. I hate looking at them because they remind me of what I have done and I am never going to be able to change that. There are very few options as to how to get rid of them. It makes it really hard to deal with personal relationships because there are so many questions about how they got there. You cannot avoid talking about self-injury even though it may be something that you have left in your past.

During the summer I still avoid swimming which I used to love because I don't want the questions and judgment from others. Even if someone knows what you have been through, they will still look. We are human and people tend to stare at things that are abnormal. This problem is even worse if you have carved a word(s) into your skin. I carved the word "fat" into my skin on two different occasions and locations. I also carved the word "failure."

There is a sentence on my leg that says, "I am fucking worthless." Can you imagine how your boyfriend or girlfriend might react when they see these words on your skin? How do you make someone understand that you were in a totally different mindset when you were cutting words into yourself? It is a mindset filled with self-loathing and it is one that I wish I could take back now. But I can't because now those words are virtually tattooed on my skin.

In closing, I would like to say that I recognize people self-injure for a reason and when you are in the midst of the behavior, you are not thinking about the consequences. I encourage parents to not avoid the problem. It is so important to get help as soon as possible so the consequences are not as severe. The longer you ignore the problem, the worse the damage will be later. I have now been self-injury free one year. I have chosen to quit for myself and I do not plan on ever going back.

MORGAN, AGE 19

I know most people can remember the first time they cut themselves with great clarity, but I cannot. On numerous occasions, I have tried to remember when this all started for me, but the memory has never come back. It is as if I have blocked it out of my mind, but that is not that uncommon for me. I block a lot of things out of my mind. I have been told by many that this is my way of coping with distressing thoughts. Maybe this is because I did not have a great childhood.

My parents got divorced when I was four years old. My dad moved out of our house and directly into his girl-friend's house (who is now my stepmother). She had three of her own kids so when my dad left the house, he also left the family. It was as if he replaced one life with another. His new family lived in our neighborhood, which meant his new kids went to the same school as us. I say "us" because I have two older siblings. Living so close to us and attending school functions with his new kids would make one think that he would also attend them for us. Unfortunately, this was not the case. His new wife was uncomfortable with my dad being around my mom so he avoided us even at school functions.

I won't bore you with all the details, but I will say that it was incredibly painful to see my dad lovingly escort his new daughter to our middle school's father-daughter dance. He saw me there with my uncle and looked away. He then spent the rest of the night avoiding eye contact with me and making sure he was always on the other side of the room. Conversely, I couldn't take my eyes off of him. He looked so happy as he danced with her, talked to her, and laughed with her. I couldn't help but wonder what was wrong with me. Why didn't he want me in his life? Why didn't he want to dance, talk, or laugh with me? Why did she get to have a dad and why did mine leave? Oddly, I never felt angry with him. I just felt confused, sad, and lonely.

I know more now then I knew then. Feeling sad and lonely was one of the reasons that I cut and burned myself. It was a way for me to feel better. I know it sounds strange, but it lifted my mood. It took away my sadness. I did not feel anger. I avoided this feeling because I was afraid that if I got mad, I would never have a chance at a relationship with my dad. After all, who wants to spend time with someone who is filled with anger and hatred toward you? I was convinced that this is why my dad did not spend time with my older siblings. They were furious with him and had no problem sharing their feelings with him.

Just like I avoided my anger, I avoided my pain every time I hurt myself. Interestingly, I usually burned my skin when I was feeling anger and cut when I was feeling sad or lonely. I combined the two and/or hit myself with my fists when I blamed myself for things in my life, including my father leaving our family. Self-injury was often a way for me to punish myself for not being good enough, not being loveable enough, and not being smart enough. I would literally beat myself up for being bad. In all of these cases, no matter if I cut, burned or punched myself, I found a great release from the tension and distress that I was experiencing.

I self-injured several times a day for many years. It was very difficult to stop because it was the one thing that made me feel good. It wiped my pain away. I would sometimes hurt myself impulsively, but most of the time, I planned out how and when I would mutilate my body. I also planned out how I would care for my wounds after I inflicted them on myself. Some people have asked me if this is because I did not want scars. The answer has always been "no." I think this was really true because back then, I did not mind my scars. They each told a story about my life. I liked having a constant reminder of the tough times in my life and a scar to show how I got through that tough time. For example, following the father-daughter dance, I went home and hurt myself. Although the black and blue marks have faded long ago on my inner thighs (from punching myself), the scar on my shoulder (from cutting) and the scar on my foot (from burning) remained. For years, they reminded me of the pain I experienced that night and my ability to cope with that pain.

Looking back now and writing this down for many to read, I realize that the way in which I coped was not good. However, in my mind, it was still an achievement, a victory. When I talked with my therapist about this, I remember thinking how crazy I must sound. Who would enjoy having scars? Who else would see hurting themselves as an achievement? I just knew that I felt pain and couldn't deal with it verbally, so I dealt with it physically.

My therapist shared a quote with me written by someone who cut. The person wrote, "How will you know I am hurting, if you cannot see my pain, to wear it on my skin, tells what words cannot explain." I think this is brilliantly written. It is exactly what I was thinking and feeling. It is hard to tell people that you are in pain or to even admit it to yourself. Instead, it is easier to show it to yourself and to others.

I wish the quote had something in it about scars and how they do not always remind a person of their pain, but of their victory and how they overcame their distress. Perhaps this is the difference between people who like to see their scars and do not want to get rid of them and those who see them as a painful reminder of a very dark time in their lives. These people seem to want to get rid of them and are devastated to see the marks on their body every day. I fit into the former category. I suppose this could change for me one day. I am not sure how my future employer, husband, children, etc., will respond to seeing these scars. I guess I will have to cross that bridge when I get to it.

For now, I have a good perspective on why I hurt myself and why I chose to stop. I was highly motivated to enter treatment. I found a therapist on my own and drove myself to my first appointment. In treatment, I learned other ways to deal with my distress. I learned how to find peace in my life by finding other coping mechanisms. I also learned how to identify things that trigger me. When I feel rejected or abandoned by someone, I have the urge to cut. When someone treats someone else unfairly, I have the urge to burn. When I do not get positive reinforcement for something that I am proud of because I have worked hard on it, I feel the urge to hit myself.

I have been in recovery for two years now. I am in college and doing very well. I still struggle with occasional urges to time to hurt myself, but they do not consume my life anymore. I take each day at a time. I want to say I will *never* injure myself again, but that might not necessarily be true. I am aware that with recovery comes relapse. In the beginning of my recovery, I relapsed over seven times (during my first year). However, I have been self-injury free for one year now and what I can say truthfully is that I never want to go back to where I was before. I cannot beat myself up over the choices I made, all I can do is try my best to take care of myself in healthy and functional ways. Thank you for listening to my story.

CANDICE, AGE 21

My story is different from others because I did not start out with a behavior that most would consider self-injurious. Even doctors recognized my problem as something very different. It all started when I was in the fifth grade. I remember sitting in my mom's bathroom one night, on the floor, looking at myself in the mirror. While I was examining my face, I noticed that my eyelashes were uneven. I had long beautiful eyelashes and wanted them to look right. Therefore, I trimmed them, ever so slightly, in an attempt to even them out. I started with the ones on my right eye. Unfortunately, I didn't like the result. Have you ever tried to cut your own bangs? You attempt to cut them straight, but they never quite look right (unless you are a professional of course). That is how my eyelashes looked. Although I was unhappy with what I did, I tried to forget about it and went to bed.

The next day, I examined my face in the mirror once again. As I looked at what I had done the night before, I became very unhappy with what I saw. The eyelashes on my right eye looked completely uneven; more so than they did before I tried to fix them. They also looked straight and flat instead of long and wavy. When I touched them, they felt dense and stubby. I was horrified! I kept touching them hoping that somehow they would go back to the way they were yesterday. Obviously, this did not happen. I couldn't stand the way they felt, so I decided to pull them out. There were only a few, so I didn't see the harm in it. However, there was harm in it. When I looked at myself in the mirror again, I saw that I created a gap in the line of my lashes. The area looked bare and much worse than the trim. I began to panic. I tried to cover it up with mascara, but this did not work. It only made my other lashes look thicker and longer, which in turn made the gap more noticeable. I tried to move the lashes over to fill the gap but they wouldn't stay there.

I didn't know what to do. I was embarrassed and scared. I didn't want to talk to anyone about what I did, but I needed help. I decided to go to my mother and ask her for help. She comforted me as best she could, but every time I looked in the mirror, I became filled with anxiety and started to cry. As crazy as it may sound to people, I couldn't stand the way they looked or felt, so I decided to pull the rest of my eyelashes out to make them look the same. I know that most people would have done the opposite, but I felt compelled to pull them.

Once I began pulling the rest of them out, something strange started to happen to me. I began to feel much less distraught and much more relaxed. I liked the way it felt to pull them out. Instead of giving me more anxiety, it relieved my stress. I felt calm and relaxed as well as happy and invigorated. This feeling led to my desire to pull more eyelashes out, so I did. I began pulling out the lower lashes on my right eye. Pulling out the top ones gave me inner peace; something I had not felt for awhile. I wanted to feel that way some more. It worked. I was completely relaxed.

However, this feeling did not last for long. I looked in the mirror once again and immediately felt anxious with what I saw. I looked really strange. All the eyelashes on my right eye were gone and the lashes on my left eye were intact, long, and beautiful. My anxiety was high and I knew exactly what I had to do to decrease my distress.

I sat in front of the T.V., watching a show with my sister. I began to pull out the rest of my eyelashes. It took me about two hours to get them all out. Some of them were hard to get out. I had to go to the mirror and come up with a plan of how to extract them. It was a process for me. I would look at them, feel them, and then pull them. I think this ritual is what led to my feelings of inner calm. However, I did not always feel at peace. I often felt guilty and distraught after I pulled my eyelashes out. I knew that I was doing something that was bad for me and that would be frowned upon by others. I knew people would judge me and potentially ridicule me for having no lashes especially if they found out that I was pulling them out on purpose. This distress led to more pulling. It became a vicious cycle. Every time I felt an eyelash come in, I had an urge to pull it out. I didn't like the way it felt or the way it looked standing alone. I obsessed about getting rid of my eyelashes and then felt compulsively driven to remove them. I came to find out that this problem has a name.

I was diagnosed with Trichotillomania by my doctor later that year. Trichotillomania is a DSM IV diagnosis that is exemplified by recurrent pulling out of one's hair resulting in noticeable hair loss. The person experiences an increased sense of tension immediately before pulling out the hair and when attempting to resist the behavior. In addition, the person experiences pleasure, gratification or relief when pulling out the hair.

I was stuck in this cycle for ten years until I entered treatment with a therapist that utilized specific interventions as way to try to help me change my behavior. These interventions were helpful and I was able to stop eyelash pulling for the first time in a very long time. However, this is when a new behavior developed, which has led to my interest in writing this story. I didn't realize it at first, but I began "symptom jumping." I moved from pulling my eyelashes out to biting off my taste buds. It hurt a lot, but I enjoyed the sensation of the pain. It felt satisfying. I liked being able to create the sensation of the pain and I also liked the accomplishment of the act itself. Once the pain subsided, I experienced tranquility once again.

There is no formal DSM IV diagnosis for self-injurious behavior. Unlike Trichotillomania, it does not have its own criteria. Instead, it is identified as a symptom of some other major psychiatric illnesses, which I do not have. I am not as concerned with the name of what I do, but instead with the process in which I do it. The process of both (hair pulling and biting off my taste buds) are very similar for me. Although they can both be very painful, they provide me with a way to numb my distress and release my tension. Because these processes are very similar for me, I began to think about my behaviors as a way to hurt myself. I had a new understanding of what I was doing and why I was doing it. This change in mindset helped me to see how out of control I really was.

Initially, pulling and biting gave me a sense of control, but now understanding that it is a way to self-harm, I recognize that I am not in control at all. Instead, I am out of control and hurting myself in very unhealthy and unproductive ways. It is not easy for me to tell other people what I am thinking and what I am feeling. I have built a shield around me to guard myself from being hurt. I do not easily trust people. I know this is one of the reasons that I hurt myself. If I can focus on pulling or biting, then I don't have to focus on what is bothering me emotionally.

I am just beginning my treatment to resolve this problem. I know I have a long way to go, but I am motivated for the first time to stop. I don't want to continue doing what I am doing. I don't want to hide from this problem anymore. It controls a lot of what I do and interferes with me being able to just be me. I act differently because of it; I have lowered self-esteem because of it; and my self confidence is down because of it. I constantly feel like people see me as flawed. I want to put this problem behind me and have people see me for who I am. I don't want my problem to escalate. Going from hair pulling to biting off taste buds is a jump and one that provided me with more pain and increased risk for safety. This is not good for me or for my future. I know that I can change. I have faith and belief in myself. With the support of my therapist, my family, and my friends, I know I will recover!

SIERRA, AGE 14

It only hurts if I want it to -
shall I make my skin turn black and blue?
The monster inside me screams to be fed
with love from my veins, a most beautiful red.
I cannot speak about this dreaded thing
shame and despair to my heart it brings.
But when I hurt so bad after a fight,
Although I try with all my might,
I cannot help it.
I reach for the razor and when it's in my hand,
I feel so weak I cannot stand.
Yet so strong, I think I could take on the world,
Unbidden, my hand tightens, my fingers curl.
Then the rush, even better than I remember
my eyes flash, the release warm like an ember.
I protect myself with this mask,
no food, no feeling
just a razor and flask.
Then a peaceful smile that can reach for a mile,
and a girl that can sit with her fingers crossed for
awhile.
People ask about the slices I cover,
they don't understand that the cutter is my lover.
The wounds I care for meet my needs,
no one else comes close as you can see.
So how do I pull myself out of this mess,
and finally look at myself when I dress?
No more disgust with my body and scars,
only respect for my progress thus far.

Please God help me recover,
help free me from this deadly lover.
I know I can do it if I give myself the chance,
and move down my path, in song and in dance.
Happy and content with myself and my life
defeating my triggers and withstanding my strife.

MICHAEL, AGE 17

The beginning and middle of my story of self-injury
may be similar to others, but I think the ending will surprise you. I know it surprised me and left me wondering
how I got to this place in my life. It started one day when a
kid came to my school and talked in an assembly about his
experience with self-injury. As I listened, I remember
thinking he was nuts for hurting himself on purpose. Who
in the world would intentionally cut and burn themselves? It seemed completely ludicrous to me. What
seemed almost more absurd was the fact that it somehow
made him feel better. How could cutting and burning
your skin provide you with any type of good feelings? I
left the assembly, certain that this guy was crazy.

It is only now that I have walked in his same shoes that
I have a true understanding and empathy for those who
struggle with this awful problem. Self-injury ran my life
for over two years. I will never forget what started it all.

I am a very good lacrosse player. In my freshman year
of high school, I was asked to joining the varsity team. I
guess most would consider this to be a great honor. However, it quickly proved to be one of the worst things that
could have ever happened to me. There was a lot of jeal-

ousy and resentment about me being on the team and the
fact that I was the leading scorer. You would think this
would make the team happy, especially when, after several
years without winning any major tournaments, we started
a winning streak. However, because the coach wanted me
to have a lot of playing time, some of the seniors ended up
with less playing time. I understood that as a senior, not
getting the amount of playing time that they earned
through the years would be devastating. However, how
they handled their frustration was completely outrageous.
Basically, they targeted me.

Freshman year, my teammates continually picked on
me. They made my life a living hell. They stole my bike,
stole my clothes out of the locker room, and defaced my
locker. I felt a tremendous amount of pressure to avoid
altercations with my teammates and at the same time to
keep my level of play up. Most people might back down
from this pressure. They might even quit the team. However, I did not want to do this. My ultimate goal was to get
a full scholarship to an Ivy League college back east. As a
freshman, recruiters were coming out to watch games that
I was playing in. It was an incredible honor and opportunity which I was not about to screw up. So I held it
together the best that I could.

However, things were really building up inside of me.
My emotional distress was escalating every day. I told
myself I just needed to get through a couple of more
weeks and lacrosse would be over. The end of our season
was approaching and we were heading to a national com-
petition. I wanted our team to place well. I knew this

would impress recruiters and look good on my college application.

In preparation for the tournament, our coach scheduled some additional practices. Unfortunately, I had a really bad day at one of the practices. Normally, I would shrug this off, but my teammates wouldn't let it go. They rubbed it in my face for two hours during the practice and then again in the locker room. I finally had enough and I snapped. I came home infuriated and needed to find a way to get it out. I could feel the rage growing inside me. I don't know exactly what came over me. It was as if I was watching myself in a movie. I did the only thing that made sense to me at the time. While sitting on my bed, I began hitting myself with my lacrosse stick. I struck my feet, ankles and shins. At first the pain made me cringe, but then I felt calm. I liked the sensation. Every time I hit myself, a little bit of anger and frustration disappeared. I started hitting myself in other places. I hit my legs, stomach and arms. As I sat there thinking about what I was doing, I realized that I was beginning to bruise. I knew I had to make up some excuse for the bruising. Luckily, I had the best excuse in the world. I am a lacrosse player. It is a rough sport and you get knocked around by other players all the time. This notion gave me a great idea. What if I became purposely rough with other players? They would retaliate and cause me additional intentional pain; induced pain that would be socially acceptable.

Unfortunately, we did not win our tournament, but our team placed in the top 20. The season was finally over and

I was hoping to get some relief from the constant bullying. Things were a little bit better, but I quickly realized that my struggle with self-injury was not going away. I had started to hit myself any time I experienced stress. I had a lot of academic and social pressures, and I liked this new solution to all of my problems. I was only hitting myself around once a week and it wasn't hurting anyone else, so I didn't see it as a big deal. I saw it as something that was helping me, not hurting me.

Sophomore year was much more difficult then freshman year. The pressures and stress I felt increased and so did my self-harm. I went from self-injuring once a week to twice a week and sometimes even more. Again, one of the major areas of stress for me was being on the lacrosse team.

That year I was named captain of the varsity team. Again, this would seem like a wonderful thing to most people, but it reignited the negativity that I experienced among teammates the year before. The seniors were outraged. Our school, unlike most others, does not have the team vote for captain. Instead, the coach makes the decision. I told the coach that I did not want to be captain and that I thought the seniors were more deserving of this title, but the damage was already done and the rumors already flowing. I heard people whispering about the fact that my mother must have slept with the athletic director or our coach in order to gain me this title. I was horrified. By the end of the day, everyone at school was talking about it. It was completely humiliating and devastating to hear most of the student body speak about my mother in that way. It did not help that she is a young single mom who happens to be very beautiful.

One kid decided it would be funny to voice his opinion about my mother's sexual escapades with the athletic director and my coach during math class. I couldn't take it anymore. I jumped over my desk and tackled the kid to the ground. Of course, I was the only one who got sent to the principal's office. The principal immediately called my mother and asked her to come in for a meeting to discuss the incident. The fact that this meeting took place during school hours was not helpful and made matters worse. As my mother walked onto campus and entered the principal's office, even more rumors flew around the school. Everyone wondered if my mother was having an affair with the principal too.

These rumors lasted throughout the rest of the year. However, they did seem to die down a little bit. I thought I was past the worst of it when one day after a huge lacrosse game, a kid on the team decided to have everyone over for pizza at his house. I decided to go as I was trying to build friendships on the team. When I walked into the kid's house, the movie, *Forrest Gump*, was playing on his big screen T.V. Almost as if on cue, the scene where Forrest Gump's mother is having sex with the principal of the school so that she can get Forrest admitted there, came on. Everyone on the team immediately looked up at me from their seats and burst into laughter. "Sound familiar?" someone said. "Your mom is hotter than her," another person said. The coach was standing next to me and didn't say a word. It was as if he enjoyed the fact that a rumor about him and my mom was flying around school. Maybe he thought it gave him some sort of twisted prestige because my mom is pretty Whatever the case, I couldn't believe he did not say a word to the team.

I left the house feeling the same way I felt after that awful practice the year before. I was infuriated. I felt completely out of control. Why was this happening to me? How could I stop the pain? I grabbed a stick that I found on the street and started hitting myself with it, but the pain would not go away. When I got home I knew I needed something more. So I went to the kitchen and got the sharpest knife that I could find. I slowly made three long cuts from my chest down to my belly button. It was strange because I actually started to feel better. All the tension that I was holding inside of me for months seemed to disappear with the blood that oozed out of my body. Hurting myself at the time, was the only thing that made me feel better and from that first time on whenever something bad happened to me, I'd run right for the closest knife and start cutting. This is when things started to get more complicated. My behavior getting more frequent, and turning into something much more dangerous. Cutting became what I needed.

I desperately wanted to hide to my cuts from others. I knew if anyone found out they would label me as some crazy headcase. After all, this is how I labeled the kid that came to talk at our school assembly my 8th grade year. I knew if my mom found out she would completely freak out. I knew if my coach or teammates found out they wouldn't understand. In order to keep it a secret, I couldn't change in the locker room. If people saw the fresh wounds and old scars on my body they would know what I was doing. I felt compelled to avoid this at all costs. It's next to impossible to hide long intentional cuts strategically placed on your body the way you can hide bruises that could happen simply from playing a rough sport.

I avoided the locker room for the rest of the season. However, on one eventful evening, I was unable to do so. In order to make it to an awards ceremony, I had to use the locker room after a tournament game. I needed to shower, change, and get across town as soon as possible. I didn't want anyone to see me so I waited until everyone had left the locker room before I entered. I quickly undressed and got ready to jump in the shower, when I saw out of the corner of my eye, one of my teammates staring at me. It was someone I had been friends with since kindergarten.

He approached me and said that he has been having suspicions about my self-injurious behavior for a long time. He told me that his older sister struggled with this problem for many years. He explained how devastating it was for her and the whole family to see her intentionally harm herself. He told me he understood why people did this and that he wanted to help. I tried denying that I had a problem, but it was no use. He was practically an expert. As he told me about his sister, I felt like he was talking about me. He described everything I did and why I was doing it.

I finally admitted that I hurt myself often on purpose. He saw how out of control the behavior was with me as he looked at the scars all over my body. He encouraged me to tell my mom immediately, so that I could get into some counseling. He made me promise that I would tell her that night. He said if I didn't tell her that he would. After much debate, I finally told him I would, but he didn't believe me, so he made me call her from the locker room. I didn't want to tell her that way. I chickened out when she answered the phone, but I gave my friend my word that I would talk to her later that evening in person. With that promise, he left the locker room.

I sat on the bench for a while in a daze. There were a million things racing through my mind. Was he going to tell anyone? Were more rumors going to circulate around the whole school about me? Was I going to walk onto campus tomorrow and have people stare at me and call me a freak? Was my mom going to understand? Was she going to blame me and think I was nuts? What if my coach found out? What if other teammates found out or my teacher and friends? I began to panic. I could feel the tension build. I had to do something. I had to cut. I couldn't find anything in the locker room to use. That's when I saw a light on in the athletic director's office. I walked up to his office and saw that nobody was inside. There was a knife lying on his table next to a half-eaten birthday cake on his desk. I went to open the door to his office, but it was locked. I had to get that knife. I could see it through the window, but I couldn't get to it.

Something came over me and I was determined to get inside. I grabbed my lacrosse stick and I broke the window. I reached through the glass and opened the door from inside. As I unlocked the door, I felt a piece of broken glass cut my arm. It immediately made me feel better. I saw a piece of glass on the floor and grabbed it, so that I could cut some more. I felt totally out of control. I began cutting my legs. I started on the tops of my thighs and then moved toward my inner thighs. I sat on the floor of his office and watched the blood come out of me. My tension seemed to leave me along with the blood. I remember starting to feel light headed and dizzy and then things went black.

The next thing I remembered was lying in a hospital bed. My mother was sitting next to me crying and holding my hand. A doctor and nurse were talking to each other at the foot of my bed. I could not hear what they were saying. When they saw that I was awake, they came over to talk to me. The doctor informed me that I lost consciousness due to significant blood loss. He said that if my friend did not go back into the locker room that night to find me, I would have died. He said that my friend saved my life. I couldn't believe what happened. It was never my intention to die.

I was discharged from the hospital with 46 stitches. I did not play in the end of the season tournament. Our team did not make it to nationals that year. Upon my discharge from the hospital, I entered intensive treatment for my self-injurious behavior. What happened to me that night gave me the strength and motivation to change.

Through a lot of therapy, I learned how to voice my pain and better deal with my emotional distress. My self-injury was no longer my voice. I was able to successfully stop hurting myself and I plan to keep that way. I agree that my friend saved my life that night. However, I also believe being in treatment saved it too. I thank my mother every day for supporting me through my treatment and now through my recovery. I couldn't have done it without her. I hope that you find the help for your child that he/she needs before it is too late. Thank you for listening to my story.

KAYLEE, AGE 16

My first memory of hurting myself was when I was in the 4th grade. I remember one hot summer day walking outside of my house on the street. The asphalt was extremely hot and I burned the bottoms of my feet. At first, I didn't like the feeling because it was so hot, but then I found it comforting in some way. I distinctly remember telling myself not to move. Eventually, the pain of the heat dissipated and I felt calm. After that first time, I continued to go out to the street often as a way to punish myself. Each time, I got a strange positive feeling that came from this burning sensation. My feet were bright red and it would hurt to walk afterwards, but I didn't care. I really believed I deserved to be punished even if I did not really do anything wrong.

My next memory of hurting myself was when I was in the sixth grade. I was in the midst of a lot of family turmoil. I couldn't handle the chaos and dysfunction, so I started biting myself to take the focus off my emotional pain. I wanted to put the focus onto something physical. Once it became physical, I needed to get rid of that pain too. I got really good at numbing the physical pain. Being able to do this gave me some control. I felt like I had absolutely no control in my life. My family was out of control, my emotions were out of control, and I felt completely helpless. The biting helped me escape from all of that. For the first time in a long time, I felt powerful.

At first I bit my arms and then my hands. The bite marks caused noticeable bruising. People started inquiring if someone grabbed me or hurt me in some way. I had to make up an excuse so my parents would not be suspicious. I told them that I hit my arm on a jungle bar out on the playground.

My next memory is when I was in the 7th grade. I was feeling incredibly depressed and began cutting. I got creative and took apart pencil sharpeners and then used the blades to self-injure. I also tore apart shaving razors. I was cutting alot. I cut at school, at home, and at friends' houses. I graduated from my own devices and started buying razor blades from the art store. By the end of 7th grade I was cutting up to 100 times per day. In know many of you reading this may think I am exaggerating, but I am not. In a very short period of time, I cut multiple times in multiple places. It escalated quickly from 10 times a day to 20 then 40 then 80 then up to 100. I used to count the amount of cuts I made on my skin the way someone with anorexia would count her calories. The cuts were on my arms, legs, and stomach. They started off shallow and grew to be deep. I never got stitches but I am pretty sure on more than one occasion I needed some. I generally cut on new places of skin. However, there were times that I cut on the same wound because there was little skin left untouched, since I was cutting so regularly.

After I cut, I would care for my wounds and make sure that they were healing correctly and not getting infected. My ritual was to wash off the blood with water and a paper towel. I would then cover them with gauze and medical tape. I would check on my wounds daily to make sure they were healing properly and safely. I then covered them with my clothing to protect them and hide them from others. As you can see, it was a process for me to harm myself and then care for myself. Caring for my wounds gave me a purpose. It was one of the only ways I took care of myself. In fact, it was the only way I ever felt cared for. I was in complete control of creating a wound and then caring for that wound. This process was very symbolic for me in my treatment and recovery.

I was always worried about being labeled and misunderstood for my self-injurious behavior. I believe that a lack of understanding, often translates into lack of communication about the problem itself. People avoid what frightens them. That is one of the reasons that I am sharing my story in this book. I want people to be educated about self-injury. Self-injury is not a joke or a superficial problem. Disrespecting someone with this problem or mistreating them due to ignorance or fear is highly detrimental. I know people can be incredibly mean, but they need to understand that self-injury is a devastating problem that can take over a person's life. Initially, the person is afraid to stop the problem because they don't want to give up their coping mechanism. However, this usually changes over time. The person eventually realizes that self-injury really isn't helping them. They want to stop, but often cannot on their own. It is importantto get into treatment to receive the help that they need.

Although every teenager is different, I believe that when a parent approaches their kid about entering treatment and getting help, it should be done in a loving, supportive, and cautious way. Anger, frustration, resentment and blame are not helpful and can ultimately push your child away. It may also make them resent treatment and not want to get help. Conversely, they might stick with what they know works for them – their self-injurious behavior. Lastly, I think parents need to be aware that there is no "quick fix" solution to self-injury. It will not go away in a few weeks. Instead, a gradual shift takes place in the way that the person deals with their distress. This change takes time. Parents should respect this process and be patient with their child during treatment and recovery.

SUSAN, SINGLE MOM

My daughter, Emily, struggled with self-injury for over three years. She explained to me that self-injury had nothing to do with wanting attention. In fact, for her it seemed like the exact opposite. She would do anything to hide what she called, "those embarrassing marks," even if it meant forgoing a family vacation in Hawaii. She made up incredible tales to avoid suspicion and recognition, but eventually her stories were too much. Even the most oblivious parent would become suspicious. How many rose bushes can you fall into? How many times can the cat scratch up your arm? Especially when the cat did not seem to do this to any other family member. How many times can you run into a pole at school and fall off your bike?

When questioned about her stories, she would make them even more elaborate. If questioned further, she would become defensive and turn things around on us, saying that we didn't trust her or that we always favored our oldest and youngest daughters over her. Emily also tried to hide her scars from her friends. Many of them would call me and leave me messages of concern. Several of her friend's parents called as well to let me know that they had seen the scars or scratches. I found myself becoming quite the storyteller along with my daughter. I think I did this for three main reasons. I wanted to believe she was telling the truth, I didn't want to admit there was a problem, and I wanted to protect her privacy.

One day I walked into my daughter's room and found her sitting on the floor with her legs crossed and her arms bleeding. She was holding an X-Acto knife in one hand and a tissue in the other. She was sitting on a towel which covered the carpet. It looked like she was about to per-form a surgery. She had a tissue box, a stack of small towels, Neosporin, and a handful of Band-Aids all neatly arranged in front of her. This was not an impulsive act for her, but rather something she had planned out meticulously. I was horrified, disgusted, confused, and fascinated all at the same time. When I entered the room, her back was facing me. She heard the door open and suddenly swung her head around. She clearly did not expect me. She looked up at me and I instead of seeing my 14-year-old daughter sitting in front of me, I saw my 6-year-old child. Her eyes widened and filled with tears. It was the same look she used to give me when she knew she did something wrong that was going to get her in trouble. She stared into my eyes and did not move.

I walked toward her and knelt down beside her. I wasn't sure what to do. She was bleeding and shaking. I did what I always did when she was frightened or hurt; I took her in my arms and held her close to me. She started to cry and I tried to comfort her and tell her that everything was going to be okay. I don't know how long we sat there together, but it seemed like an eternity. Eventually, we got her cleaned up and bandaged. Her wounds were superficial and she did not need stitches. She was not able to talk to me that night and I didn't push her to. This was partly selfish because I don't think I wanted to hear what she had to say. All I kept thinking in my mind is how I failed as a parent. I was afraid that I somehow caused this.

A few years ago, I divorced my girls' father. The divorce was extremely bitter. I know it affected all my girls especially Emily. Emily had been very close to her father. After the divorce, he stopped coming around. He made up a million excuses as to why he couldn't spend time with the girls. Emily hated all of the excuses and stories. She knew he was hiding something and she despised the fact that he would not just tell the truth. However, she did the same thing. She also made up excuses and elaborate stories to cover up the truth about her problem with self-harm. Maybe this made her feel closer and more connected to her father in some way. In any case, it was hard not knowing the truth sooner.

Once I was aware of what was going on with Emily, I was able to get her the help she needed. I did a lot of research to find the right therapist. I recommend that parents interview a variety of therapists first before they have their child meet with one. I think it is important for parents to feel comfortable with the person who will be working with their child. It also important to make sure there is a good connection between the therapist and your child. I think a lot of parents have a sense of the type of personality that would match with their child's. This saved my daughter from having to meet with a lot of people and instead gave her a choice of two or three. I narrowed down my search pretty quickly because I was determined to find someone with true expertise in self-harm. I asked each therapist how often they met with patients who suffered from this problem; what their treatment approach was, and what their success rate was with their patients.

In the end I found a wonderful therapist who was able to work with my daughter both individually and in a group setting. This dual type of intervention seemed to work well for her. In her individual therapy sessions, she was able to get the one-on-one attention she needed to resolve conflict and minimize her distress. In her group therapy

sessions, she was able to talk with others who also struggled with self-harm and work with them to find alternative
coping mechanisms.

My daughter has been free from self-harm for over 18
months. She admitted to me one night that although her
self-injury was never about wanting attention, there were
moments in her life that she felt like pulling up her sleeves
and screaming to people, "Look at me!" Maybe that is
why she left her bedroom door unlocked the day that I
found her. She needed me to see and to know and to help
her stop. I am glad that she received the help she needed.
She says avoiding self-harm is a constant personal battle.
However, I am convinced with the support system she has
in place, including her therapist, her group, her friends,
her siblings, and yes me, her mother, she will continue to
find alternative ways to cope. I love my daughter and I am
so very proud of her.

HILLARY, AGE 15

I grew up in a very hectic family with three older
brothers and parents who fought constantly. My brothers
all drank, and my middle brother was into just about every
hard drug imaginable. Since I was the little girl my mom
always wanted, and the baby of the family, she was very
protective of me.

Growing up in this household I always felt pressure to
be perfect in order to make up for the mistakes that my
brothers made. Because of this, I never had anyone to talk
to about the drug and alcohol abuse I was around or the
sexual abuse I endured from my oldest brother. My

parents thought I was too young to remember and that none of these issues would stay with me. However, I have vivid memories of fights between family members starting at the age of five. By sixth grade, as a result of all this stress, I became bulimic. It was one thing I felt that I could control. I struggled with an eating disorder for approximately one year. When I was in seventh grade, my teacher found out about my eating disorder and said I had to stop or she would talk to my parents. I didn't want my parents to find out, so I stopped. However, my stress level grew and I needed another way to cope.

During that time, I had a best friend who cut. She told me how much it helped her to deal with the stress and pressure she experienced in her life. I decided to try it. At first, I tried scratching my thighs and upper arms with safety pins. It gave me the same sense of control as bulimia did. However, this time I also felt a high. I knew one thing for sure, the pain was taking all of my problems away.

Soon the small scratches weren't giving me the same high that I once got from them, so I started breaking apart razors and using the blades to self-injure. These bigger cuts helped me focus on the pain I was experiencing on the outside, rather than the pain I was feeling inside. Self-injury made me feel powerful. It gave me a sense of mastery because I could numb my emotional distress. However, by numbing it, it got worse. I began to have suicidal thoughts. I was becoming really depressed. My self-injury was getting worse and I was spiraling out of control. I real-

ized I was in trouble, but by that time I was in too deep to
care.

Luckily, I had a softball coach who became a mentor to
me. I trusted her and decided to tell her about all of the
things that were going on in my life including my problem
with cutting. Unfortunately, I think it freaked her out
because she began to ignore me. After a few months of
avoiding me, I was called into the principal's office. I
found out that my coach decided to tell my school principal everything I had disclosed to her. She also decided
to tell my mother that I had done something horrible and
was now in trouble. She refused to give my mother further
detail.

That day my mom picked me up from school in a
panic. She thought I was pregnant. When I told her I was
not pregnant and that I cut, she responded, "How many
times?" I was confused and told her I had no idea. I
quickly realized she thought I was cutting school. She had
no idea that I was cutting my skin. I think the idea of me
intentionally hurting myself was incomprehensible to her.
Once I cleared up what I meant by "cutting," she went ber-
serk. She started screaming at me. I didn't know what to
do. I was no longer her "perfect" little girl.

My mother immediately put me into counseling. I did
not feel comfortable talking to my first counselor. It was
not a good match for me at all. She told my parents things
that should have been kept confidential, so I didn't trust
her. During most sessions, we sat and played board games
instead of working on my problems. She suggested different coping mechanisms like snapping rubber bands on

my skin, squeezing ice cubes, and keeping a log of how many times I cut per day. The problem with the rubber bands was that it still allowed me to self-injure. I had huge welts on my arms. The problem with the ice cubes was that it only made my hands numb, which pissed me off even more. The problem with the cutting log was that it turned into a mental game for me. By counting the amount of times that I cut every day with no understanding as to why this was important, I just ended up cutting more. After months of working with this therapist and faking sick so I didn't have to see her, I finally got up the courage to tell my parents that I didn't like her and was not getting anything out of the sessions. I told them that I needed to find someone new.

My dad's co-worker suggested my current therapist. After the very first session, I got closer to solving my problems than I ever had been with my previous counselor. The whole time I knew that the only person that could make me stop was me. However, having the right person to work with was very important because I knew that I could not do it on my own. I remember clearly what finally made me want to stop cutting. It was during my eighth grade year. I was at a soccer game. I was sitting with a friend and a girl saw fresh cuts on my skin. With a look of disgust on her face, she asked me what they were. This is when I realized that cutting was beginning to define me and how others viewed me. I did not want to be labeled as a "cutter." I wanted to learn how to control my emotions. I wanted to learn how to stop cutting.

With my therapist's help, I found other coping mechanisms that were much more helpful. I had to learn more about myself to see what could make me happy both externally and internally. I realized that when I laughed, I automatically felt better. I started surrounding myself with friends, listening to music, and watching entertaining television shows like *Family Guy* to make me laugh. To let out anger, I bought a punching bag, went on runs, and worked out. I channeled my anger into my sport. I am a softball player who perfected her game.

My advice to those who cut is to get help as soon as possible. Self-injury can quickly escalate. Confide in someone you can trust. Realize that there are positive coping mechanisms to release pain like working out, journaling, blasting your favorite music, watching hilarious shows and movies, reading, or spending time with friends. It is also important to identify the underlying reasons for your distress. I believe that in order to recover successfully from self-injury, these issues need to be addressed in counseling. This insight-oriented therapy was very helpful for me. It is what helped me to understand my pain, and not just how to fix it.

I know a lot of parents are reading this book. If you are trying to help your child stop cutting, make sure that you are supportive. It is important to remain calm when you find out that she is cutting. Do not flip out and scream at her. Offer to listen to her and help.

If you are embarrassed or ashamed of her for cutting, try not to show it. Acting like cutting is something you need to hide creates a lot of shame and guilt for the person with the problem. My parents used to come in my room in the middle of the night to look at my arms while I was sleeping. I faked like I was still asleep so I could understand what they were doing. They saw all the cuts on my body and still never had the courage to bring it up with me. They were really embarrassed by it. I felt guilty that I caused this embarrassment. I was ashamed that I was no longer their perfect little girl. These feelings led to more self-injury for me.

I think once self-injury is out in the open, parents often use it as a way to measure their child's stability. Although I understand why parents would do this (because they are worried about their kid), it is not helpful. For example, if you notice that your kid is upset, it is not a good idea to immediately ask to see her arms to make sure she didn't cut. First, this feels like an invasion of privacy. Second, this feels like a set-up. If you have healing wounds, parents tend to give you the third degree to find out when and why you hurt yourself. If you have fresh cuts, parents either take it personally and blame themselves for failing you, or they become angry and yell at you for making a bad decision once again. People cut for many reasons. Relapse happens. When it does, try not to take it personally, and offer to help once again.

I am proud to say that I am self-injury free. Thanks for reading my story.

KATHERINE, AGE 24

My world became defined by my addiction to self injury when I was about 15; long enough ago for it to feel like it was a different person's memories, like a fuzzy dream right after waking. Surreal. Certainly that wasn't me – I didn't feel the immense need to cut myself every day; that makes no logical sense. If only it was true. Cutting was visceral and real in my life, and I can't just pretend it didn't happen. I wish I could, but I have the scars to show for it that I will carry with me forever.

Where to start with such a blur of a story? I let it get blurry so it is easier to live with. In all honesty, it **worked**. That's why I became addicted to it. It alleviated my pain, translated it into something tangible and visible and ruby red. For a little while. But a fix only lasts so long.

The first time I cut myself, I was in a deep depression, and I had seen scars on an acquaintance's legs from cutting – words like SLUT and FAT scarred into her thighs. I remember thinking, hey, I'm more depressed than her; I am at *rock bottom*. Then I thought, "Well if she's doing it, there must be some reason, it must work." I was desperate. I tried it, and it took a while to get the courage to really cut deeply, but once I learned how, it was a slippery slope and it was too late to go back.

I didn't do it for attention; I hid my scars, cut myself in non-obvious places. My calves are scarred permanently – everyone thinks of "cutters" as slices on the arms. I did that too, of course, but that's harder to hide. And a bit cliché. I was "different," not some emo kid torn up by my teen angst, this was **deep**. That's how I saw myself then. Special. An exception to the rule. But still worthless – an odd dichotomy that I still can't fully understand.

I was hospitalized on a 5150 after cutting my bicep too much at 16– I was scared I went too far and went to my parents about it. The hospital thought I was trying to kill myself (by cutting my bicep?) and put me on a 72 hour hold in an 18-and-under psychiatric wing. In theory, the doctors probably meant well. But this hospitalization is what sealed my addiction and made cutting a part of my identity.

The nurses put all the "Cutters" – what they labeled us – in the "cutters' room," - me and three other girls who self-injured. They made us strip down to our underwear every day to show that we didn't have new cuts. But they weren't very careful with the intake inspection, because those girls taught me more about cutting and hiding it than I ever thought possible and we bonded over this shared need. We masterminded ways to find sharp objects, shared our secret methods (the third razor in the blade is the sharpest!) and basically made each other worse.

The nurses were no help. They had labeled me a "cutter," and it made me feel like one. That was who I was, broken and unfixable - better strip-search her! The psychiatrist there? Ha. I saw him for about five minutes total in the couple of weeks I was held there. People who self-injure are probably terrifying and impossible to comprehend, so it's easy to label and medicate and pretend everything will just polish up.

Eventually the scars and my own vanity helped me stop doing it. I kept imagining myself in a wedding dress with scars on my arms, the best day of my life as a reminder of its darkest times.

I relapsed when I was 19 for about a year. I was living in a sorority house that I really didn't belong in. I was once again deeply depressed, and I had my self-injury down to a system there. I stole the big first-aid kid and kept it under my bed to treat the cuts after I made them, and stole disposable razors from the guest room to turn into instruments of self-destruction.

When my roommates weren't spending the night in our room, which was pretty frequent, I went through what turned almost into a routine of cutting, treating, hiding, cutting, treating, hiding... a very repetitive cycle.

Later I dropped out of the term and checked myself into outpatient therapy. I knew I needed help – not just with self-injury, but with my depression and the way I was escaping it. Self-injury was one major way, but I vacillated between that and abusing alcohol or eating-disordered behaviors of extreme restriction. All were cut from the same cloth, and all were attempts to escape my emotional pain.

I started to want desperately to stop. This inner determination is what I believe helped me quit hurting myself. Everyone's story is completely different, and people don't self-injure for the same reasons. Nor do they stop for the same reasons. What worked for me was, along with having a caring family, envisioning my future and making the decision that I did not want to scar myself permanently, making the secret shame public for all to see. Even on my wedding day.

KELLY, AGE 22

I was 12 years old when I began a long and degrading relationship with self-injury. It all started when my best friend in middle school began cutting, then during a suicide attempt, named me as one of the main reasons for why she did not want to live anymore. She said I was a horrible friend and a terrible person. I was crushed and distraught. When I got home from school that day, I remember going to my mother's bathroom, meticulously taking apart a razor and exposing a single blade. As I dragged the razor across my skin, I felt a strange release. I experienced numbness and comfort. I sat in completely quiet on the bathroom floor and watched the blood drip down my forearm and onto my wrists. I thought of how I would explain the cuts while I remembered the words of my best friend. The next five years would be filled with long sleeves, shame, and detachment.

Earlier that year, my "so called" best friend and I had been walking her dog when she suddenly kicked me in the shin. As she watched the blood run down my leg she looked me in the eye and said "I have always wanted to see you bleed." She then chased me six blocks home and began pounding on my door saying she wanted to beat me up. My parents told her to leave as I hid, curled up into a ball, under the table crying. That was my first abusive relationship.

One year later, at the age of 13, I remember asking my mother for help. We were sitting alone on the couch watching television. I showed her my cuts and told her what I was doing to myself. She said she would help. I felt a strange sense of relief. Unfortunately, I would not see this help until around age 15. It was not brought up again. It was as if my confession was lost somewhere in translation. I would spend most nights sitting in my room with a razor blade, rubbing alcohol, and a bandage in my hand. I listened to depressing music while I cut myself then diligently cared for my wounds.

I spent a lot of time thinking about how I got to this point. I had always been a good athlete. I played high level soccer from the age of five until the age of 17. Soccer was always a priority for me. I didn't want anyone to find out that I was intentionally hurting myself so I tried to hide it from my teammates and coach. I would cut in places that they could not detect. I would not change in the locker room around anyone. One time, I put on my uniform and realized that some of my cuts showed. In a panic, I tried to cover them up by drawing over them with sharpie. It worked and nobody suspected a thing.

After that, I made sure to cut designs into my arm when self-injuring so that if I needed to use the sharpie again, it would not look like a cover up, but instead an intentional drawing. My coach thought I was weird, but he let it go because I was a good player. I can only imagine what bystanders were thinking when I walked out onto the field. I am sure I became known as the girl with jet black hair and sharpie drawn all over her inner left arm. Eventually, I couldn't hide my cuts anymore. My problem with self-harm became so debilitating that I was forced to quit my nationally-ranked team. This is when I gave up my dream of playing soccer in college.

Soccer was not the only thing that I was good at. I was an honors student and popular with all the different cliques at school. I always had a smile on my face hiding from everyone my true pain. I hid behind long sleeves and cover-up makeup. I worked hard to conceal the truth except from a select few. In middle school it was pretty simple. I had my set of friends and could hide my cutting from everyone pretty easily.

Entering high school posed some new challenges. It was extremely stressful for me. The transition to a new school was a shock. I had to make new friends, which meant new people to hide my behavior from. By my sophomore year, I started to get tired of hiding my problem.

One night, I got up the courage to confront my mother about why she never helped me. I took her out onto our front porch and pulled up my sleeve. My eyes immediately filled with tears. I asked her why she never followed through on her promise. I wanted to know why when I asked her for help, she turned her back on me. I wanted her to explain to me why I was not worth saving. Her response was that she did not know what to do. She told me that she knew nothing about self-injury and had absolutely no idea of how to go about helping me. She admitted that she hoped the problem would simply go away. Unfortunately for both of us, it did not. However, fortunately, this time my mother took action. She began researching the problem and found me an expert in the field to work with. I had my first individual therapy appointment when I was 15 years old.

This was the same age I was when I met my first boy-friend. He was a senior in high school and the captain of the wrestling team. He was absolutely perfect in my teenage eyes. Little did he know what he was getting into when he started dating me. I was a bipolar girl with a pretty smile and a tortured soul. We were together for three years, and during that time, we went through a lot together. He attended my very first therapy appointment with me. He wanted me to get help. He knew I was cutting myself several times per day. He witnessed the intensity of my pain and how I dealt with it physically. He wanted me to talk about it, but I couldn't. Not back then anyway.

There was one situation that really frightened him. It frightened me as well. I remember it like it was yesterday. It was during my junior year. My boyfriend and I got into a fight. We were in my bedroom screaming at each other over something really stupid. The next thing I knew, I was standing in the kitchen in a pool of my own blood. I remember the kitchen floor feeling really cold. I looked down at my body and saw that I had a steak knife in my hand and a cut down the center of my thigh. I had no rec-ollection of how I had gotten there. My boyfriend and mom told me what had happened. I was shocked. How could I not remember cutting myself?

When I went to the doctor, I found out that I dissoci-ated during my self-injurious behavior. Unfortunately, this was not the only time that this happened to me. There were other times as well. On another occasion, my boyfriend walked in on me while I had a knife in my hand.

He says I was standing in the kitchen, same steak knife in hand, mumbling something along the lines of "you'll never be good enough you stupid, fat, unlovable, piece of…", as I ran it swiftly from left to right across my left wrist. He shook me. He could tell I was not in my right state of mind. I remember looking at him, feeling panicked, and unable to recall what I was doing. I fell to the floor crying, apologizing for my entire life in one long monologue that probably lasted ten minutes. When I dissociated, I often blacked-out and had no memory of what had occurred. Other times, I felt as if I was watching myself from above, like an out-of-body experience.

This was the point when I realized my self-injury was out of control. In a dissociative state I could not control myself. There were times that I tried. I remember screaming at myself to stop the behavior, but being unable to get my body to do so. I remember worrying, "What if I accidentally kill myself?" I wouldn't even know what I had done. I did know that I didn't want to die. It was at this moment that I became motivated to get help. I was in therapy, but not really invested in getting better. Initially, I was not ready to give up the only coping mechanism that was working for me. What I knew then and I still know now, is that it was not really working for me at all.

I began to realize that self-injury was causing me to lose everything that was once important to me. I wasn't playing soccer anymore, at least not at the level that I was accustomed to. I was isolating from my friends, despite my positive demeanor and social nature. I was putting tremendous stress and strain on my relationships with my

parents and my boyfriend. I felt broken, dejected, and
alone. I was cutting at least 50 cuts a day, on my arms,
legs, and stomach. It was time to stop!

I began to work in therapy. However, therapy was
confusing. I was told by various therapists to do different
things to aid in treatment and recovery. Most of these
things were unhelpful and sometimes even stupid. One
therapist told me to wear rubber bands on my wrists, and
snap them every time I had the urge to cut. I snapped
those rubber-bands so hard, I made wounds as bad as the
ones I often made when cutting. Another suggestion was
to draw red lines where I wanted to cut. I guess this was
supposed to stop the actual behavior and satisfy the urge.
I found this suggestion stupid because my distressing feelings were still there and it was frustrating to walk around
with red lines all over my body. I already faced the humiliation of having to draw on myself to cover up my cuts.
Why would I intentionally do that now as part of my
recovery?

Eventually, I did get into the right therapist who
worked with me both individually and in groups. She
taught me that self-injury was a behavior that I had
chosen, and even though it had taken away my sport, and
many of my friends, it was not my identity. I was not a
"cutter," I was a person, and I could choose other coping
methods and leave this destructive behavior behind me.
Understanding that made a huge difference. When you
feel that you are a "cuttter," and nothing more, it is hard to
see how you can ever be anything else. Seeing self-injury

as a behavior was a much more powerful perspective for me.

My journey through treatment and recovery was gradual. I am proud to say that I have been recovered from self-injury for six years and I will be graduating from UC Berkley with my degree in psychology. I am graduating with honors and will be achieving my goal. In addition, I received early admission into a clinical doctorate program for psychology. I will begin attending this university in the fall.

I hope that my story illustrates that anyone can recover from self-injury with the right support. Compassion from loved ones, help from the right mental health professionals, and some patience and motivation are what it takes to achieve a successful recovery.

KELLY'S MOM

Before my daughter was born, I received the best advice ever from a close friend. It came from a story she shared with me about an exchange she had with her daughter the night before. My friend's fifteen-year-old daughter had crawled into bed with her and asked for help obtaining birth control. She said that she and her boyfriend decided they were going to have sex. Hearing this declaration, my friend held her breath and tried not to react until her daughter finished asking her for her support. The two of them agreed that the decision was probably not the best, but since her daughter was determined to go forward and engage in sexual activity, my friend agreed to help. She offered to take her daughter to the

doctor for counseling and birth control. I gasped as I listened, and asked her how she kept herself from forbidding
her daughter to ever leave the house again. My friend told
me that, in her opinion, the key to a strong relationship
between a teenager and a parent is being able to listen
with judging or reacting negatively to what the child says.
She told me that when faced with a stressful, upsetting,
and/or frightening situation with your child, the best
thing to do is take a deep breath, listen to what she has to
say, and resist a judgmental knee-jerk reaction.

So here my story begins ... .

When my daughter was born a bit premature, she was a
tiny beautiful gift who blessed our family. She grew into a
bright, happy girl who was always singing and skipping
through the house with her long pony tails bouncing
behind her. She was eager to help with chores and loved
to cook and work in the garden with me. She confidently
carried on conversations with older folks and always
seemed comfortable in her skin. She went off to pre-
school excited to meet new people and to learn. Kindergarten and early elementary school were a breeze for her.
In hindsight, the only thing I noticed that was a bit odd
and out of place with her normal behavior was that I
couldn't visit her at school in the middle of the day
without triggering a huge meltdown. If she had continued
down her happy path, I would never have looked back so
longingly on those days.

My daughter encountered multiple transitions when
she went in to the sixth grade. She moved from her elementary school into a middle school located in our neigh-

borhood. This meant that she had to move away from friends she had since pre-school. At the same time, she left my sister's day care, where she had spent time since infancy. In addition, her beloved soccer team folded, and her friends on the team, who attended many different schools, scattered. To make things even harder, she was not getting along with her father. All of this seemed to weigh on her as she went off to for her first day of sixth grade.

It was from this point that things in Kelly's life began to go downhill. She started to struggle to get herself to school in the morning. She would call me at work to tell me that she couldn't bring herself to leave the house and make the one block walk to school. Remembering her pain and not knowing what to do for her brings me to tears even today. I spoke with her pediatrician, who told me to be strong. She instructed me to drive her to school and tell her that she needed to go into the building. This became a horrible battle. Often, Kelly would not get out of the car on her own accord. I had to walk her into the school and then coax her into staying. Thank goodness, I was able to leave her in the hands of a kind-hearted office assistant. After dropping her off, my drives to work were torture. I did not know what was happening. Was my baby girl sad, angry, or distraught? As soon as I got to work, I would call the office assistant and check in on her. Some days were good, and some were bad. Either way, I felt like a failure. I didn't know what to do for my child or who to turn to. No one else in my life seemed to have any of these things happening with their children.

My daughter also felt like she had nobody to support her. She was at a new school and trying to make new friends, but it wasn't easy. Luckily, she found out that one of her former soccer team mates attended her school. She desperately wanted friends and tried to rekindle the friendship between them. Unfortunately for my daughter, the other girl had many friends from her elementary school attending this middle school. She didn't have much time or interest in reconnecting with my daughter. However, this teammate had a friend who was interested in becoming my daughter's friend. Things seemed to go well at first. But after awhile, my daughter complained to me that the other child had physically abusive tendencies. I spoke with the school authorities who said they'd keep an eye out for any problems. My daughter was very upset that I brought this up with the school. Once again, I felt like a failure.

The school could not supervise what occurred off-campus. One day my daughter was walking with this girl when, for no apparent reason, she was assaulted by her. My daughter tried to get away and the girl chased after her. Luckily she made a good decision to come home. When she arrived home she told me what happened. I told the girl to leave and promptly called her mother. The poor woman seemed to be at her wits end as to what to do with her disruptive child. My daughter was very upset with me for calling her friend's mother. She did not like that I interfered and confronted this woman. Again, I felt like a failure.

Shortly after this incident, my daughter came to me to tell me she was cutting herself. I took my friend's advice from long ago and tried my best not to react negatively. I was shocked. Although I had no real understanding of what cutting was, I could not fathom why anyone would do something like this to themselves on purpose. I asked friends and family if they had ever heard of anything like this and all I got were shocked faces and the answer "no." When I tried to learn more about why my daughter would s=do such a thing, she informed me that her abusive friend cut herself too. My first reaction was to wonder if she was engaging in this behavior as a way to keep this girl's friendship. At this point, I hadn't seen the evidence of the cutting and hadn't asked her to show me. What I did know was that my daughter became depressed, and lost her interest in other relationships, soccer and school. The abuse from this "friend" did not get better, it go worse. The girl began to cyber bully my daughter. This was yet another thing I had never encountered before, and I didn't know what to do about it. Once again, I felt like a failure.

I called my employers' EAP and they referred me to a psychologist. What a disaster!! My daughter HATED this woman and threatened to jump out of the moving car on the way to the second appointment. I then called our pediatrician in a panic and begged for help. I was terrified. They referred me to two professionals who I am certain saved my daughter's life. She began the long road to healing. Although, I was glad that she was finally in good hands and getting the help she needed, I still felt like a failure because I couldn't get her to this safe place sooner.

The cutting continued while she was learning new methods of how to deal with her distress. Every time she felt like her life was crashing down on her, the cutting escalated. It was devastating to see how other people reacted to her self-inflicted injuries. One of the saddest things for me was to see how even medical professionals reacted to her when they saw the many scars on her upper arms. I remember one time we needed to go to a pediatric cardiologist appointment. The doctor entered the room and told us he needed to take her blood pressure. He literally gasped when he put the blood pressure cuff on her tiny upper arm in preparation for the test. She was young and extremely hurt by his reaction. I was very angry that someone in his position who works with children on a daily basis could not refrain from reacting in this way. My precious child was in so much mental pain and in a split second reaction, he caused her more. It was completely unprofessional. We had a similar reaction from an emergency room doctor when my daughter was older. The doctor saw her scars and immediately assumed that my daughter was suicidal. Neither of us could believe that medical professionals could be so ignorant about this problem. I do not think they realize how much their reactions effect the person suffering. My daughter said that these reactions caused her to take some steps backward in her recovery.

I learned very quickly how much pain my daughter was in. You can't imagine what it is like to find razor blades hidden in secret places, to pick up clothes to do the laundry and find the carpet below soaked in blood, to have your precious child tell you she doesn't want to live like this and asks, why her. All I was able to do when she finally talked about her pain was take a deep breath and listen non-judgmentally. You cannot imagine either, the relief you feel when you find someone who really understands, knows what to do and partners with you to save your child's life. And you cannot imagine how proud I was of my daughter when she wore sleeveless shirts in public and let people see her scars.

It's so hard to try to take the lead and be in charge when your child is in so much pain and you have no clue how to help her. I've tried to be there for my daughter to the best of my ability. I've tried listen to everything she had to say without judging her in negative ways. I've learned to be an expert at holding my breath and not saying that everything will be ok when I can't be sure if it will from one minute to the next.

My daughter is very intelligent. She is a good person. Many people from the outside looking in have no clue what she has gone through. In fact, they have no clue as to what we have all gone through. Families are extremely affected by this problem. Parents suffer along with their kids. Thankfully, with the excellent help we found for her and with the support from people who really care, things have progressed to the point that my daughter is graduating from college in June self-injury free for many years now. She's already been accepted to graduate school. She is interested in becoming a clinical psychologist. She wants to help others who suffer as she did. I'm so proud of the strong young woman my daughter has become. I'm proud that she is so open with people about what she has gone through. I'm proud that she has shared everything with me and that she has forgiven me for my failures. I love my daughter and I am proud to say that after her hard work and commitment to treatment and recovery, she is self-injury free!

12

ABOUT THE AUTHOR

 Dr. Tonja H. Krautter is a licensed clinical psychologist as well as a licensed clinical social worker. She is dedicated to the mental health field, serving persons in need and providing them with the highest standard of care. Her expertise lies with extreme case matters such as eating disorders, self-mutilation, and sexual assault. Professionally, Dr. Krautter has been in the role of clinical supervisor, program director,

workshop leader, professor, and author. When not working she devotes her time to her family. She has been happily married for 15 years and has two beautiful sons, ages 9 and 7.

A

APPENDIX A: SPECIFIC TREATMENT OPTIONS

The topics listed below are frequently covered during the course of long-term therapy. They are utilized as a way to help the person who self-injures better understand the reasons behind her destructive behavior. Parents can encourage an exploration of these topics with their child. However, as a warning, please do not try to act as your child's therapist. Getting your child the right type of help with someone who has expertise in the area of self-injury will be vitally important to your child's success.

❋ *Tell your story* - This topic is a type of autobiography. The goal is for the person to describe, in as much detail as possible, many different events in her life. The events should begin with early childhood memories and follow a timeline to the present. The autobiography may include topics such as family (family

dynamics, emotional climate, relationships), peer
group (friends, significant others, relationships/con-
flicts), academic history, medical history, psychiatric
history (including eating problems, substance abuse,
etc.), employment history, leisure activities (hobbies,
talents, special interests), hardships or losses, trauma,
etc.

✳ *Personal Identity* - This topic helps the individual
explore the way in which she sees herself. I often ask
the person to distinguish between how she sees herself
on the inside and how she sees herself on the outside. I
also ask her to think about how others perceive her on
these two levels. In this category, the person should
identify personal strengths and weaknesses and how
these affect her coping abilities, relationships, and self-
esteem. The person should include her thoughts about
gender, race, and ethnicity. Positive thoughts about
any of these can help build self-esteem and should be
included and discussed. Negative thoughts that might
be contributing to self-hatred and self-destruction
should also be included and discussed. Lastly, the individual should address the different roles that she fulfills
in her life. Different roles exert different influences on
the person who is self-injuring. Therefore, this is worth
exploring in detail.

✳ *Role Models* - This topic includes an exploration of the
most influential female and/or the most influential
male in the person's life. This person can serve as a role
model for the person and aid in her recovery process. I
always recommend that the therapist explore with their

patient what type of positive influence this person has on her life. If the influence has been negative, the therapist should process why this individual has chosen this particular person as a role model.

* *Thoughts and Feelings Associated with Self-Injury* - This topic helps the person develop greater insight into the feelings that lead to her self-injurious behavior. Remember that, with knowledge and awareness, comes the power to change. This is a place where I pay special attention to "all or nothing" thinking patterns. As mentioned in earlier chapters, people who self-injure often do not see in shades of grey. They only see black and white, right and wrong, or good and bad extremes. Helping the individual break through this type of thinking and expand her insight is imperative for success in recovery.

* *Building Relationships* - This topic helps the person understand what is involved in building a non-superficial relationship. Derived from interpersonal therapy, a discussion of what a healthy, stable relationship looks like occurs in this section. This may be a foreign concept to the person who self-injures. Self-injury can be isolating. Often it is not until the person explores this idea that they are able to recognize that. Self-injury can destroy relationships or make them discordant. Accordingly, the ways in which this happens can be discovered and discussed. Many people who self-injure report having conflictual relationships with others, which leaves them feeling empty, lonely, and/or distrustful. These feelings in turn, often lower self-

esteem and deserve level which can lead to further self-harm.

✽ *Conflictual Relationships* - This topic is more specific than the last. If the person can identify someone who she is in conflict with and why, then she can begin to explore ways in which to handle those conflicts differently (especially if he or she is using self-injury as the primary coping mechanism).   This intervention is derived from insight-oriented therapy.

✽ *Verbal Self-Expression* - This is a very important topic. I often encourage the person who self-injures to explore ways in which she verbally expresses herself (if at all). Exploration of the lack of verbal self-expression is the key in helping the person benefit from this tool. For example, many patients talk about their fear of disappointing others or angering them with their words. This fear keeps them from verbalizing their pain, which in turn builds tension and leads to self-mutilation. Processing these fears, whether or not they are realistic, and discussing what she can do about them models positive verbal self-expression. It is important for the individual to begin to practice ways in which she can assert her thoughts and feelings to others. This process can be extremely empowering. I have found that increased verbal self-expression is often accompanied by a significant decrease in self-injurious behavior.

✽ *Critical Life Events* - This topic allows individuals to focus specifically on any trauma or loss that they have experienced in their lives. Included should be fantasies of revenge and alternative outcomes, as well as realistic ways to feel more empowered and less victimized. When discussing this topic with my patients, I pay very close attention to presence of self-blame and/or guilt. These are often precursors to self-injurious behavior. Individuals who blame themselves or experience guilt due to trauma or loss often feel a need to punish themselves and use self-mutilation as their means.

❋ *Taking Care of Oneself* - This topic helps the patient explore ways in which she can self-soothe other than self-mutilation. Some patients do not know of any other self-soothing techniques. It is here that others may need to help her explore what these could be. Parents, family teachers, and friends are wonderful resources in this regard. If a patient comes into my office oblivious to what other people do to take care of themselves, I assign them homework that involves finding out. You would be surprised how many ideas emerge from this brainstorming process. When discussing this topic, I pay close attention to my patient's deserve level. Many people who self-injure do not believe they are deserving of nurturance. Thus building self-esteem and building deserve level are two main goals in therapy for the self-injurer.

❋ *Success Journal* - I work with the individual to create a journal of successes. I ask the person to write a positive affirmation about herself and place it on the front page. I then encourage her to find motivational quotes, touching poems, and/or written material that inspire her to reach her goals and stick with recovery. It is a place where she can write about her successes and

include things that have been written to her, for her,
and about her. Anything and everything positive about
the self should be included in this journal. It is something that she can then reflect upon when feeling overwhelmed, undeserving or empty inside.

❄ *Summary of Progress* - This topic reinforces the awareness that has been built up in treatment and the
changes that have been made so far. Many of my
patients have great difficulty giving themselves credit
for their hard work in treatment. This topic encourages
that to take place. Asking the person who self-injures
to summarize their own progress often initially results
in blank stares and confusion. Frequently, they do not
track their progress or give themselves credit for the
gains made in therapy up to that point. Interestingly,
once they are able to do this, their progress seems to be
more strongly reinforced. In other words, they are
more apt to own and internalize the positive changes
they have cited as progress.

❄ *Miracle Question* - Derived from narrative therapy, this
technique allows the person who is self-injuring to
imagine what their life would be like without this
destructive behavior. In a detailed description, the
patient is asked to explore how exchanging this
behavior for healthier, less destructive coping mechanisms would change their life, including their mood,
activities, relationships, thought process, etc. From the
time the person wakes up in the morning until the time
that she goes to bed, she visualizes and describes what
her life would be like without self-injurious behavior.

It is a powerful tool that can instill hope, motivation, and commitment to change.

❋ *The Funeral* - This is a way to say good-bye to self-injury. I encourage my patients to become creative with this powerful topic. I have had patients write eulogies, throw away their favorite cutting or burning devices or plant flowers/trees in memory of this once trusted and beloved coping mechanism. I have even had a patient conduct an actual funeral service with friends and families in attendance. Remember that self-mutilation often becomes part of the individual's identity. Accordingly, saying good-bye to this behavior can be very difficult for some. Giving the person this opportunity, however, can be empowering and opens new pathways for self-definition/identity.

❋ *My Future* - This final topic helps the individual create an action plan in case urges re-arise and the temptation to self-harm becomes exceedingly high. Simply possessing such a plan can alleviate anxiety and help the person be more constructive. This plan may be created for daily, weekly or monthly use. It may include specific situations in which the patient foresees a problem. Before coming up with an action plan, the person needs to determine what she needs in order to be most successful in living without self-injury. She should outline reasonable, attainable goals for herself that will reinforce success. These goals do not have to focus on self-injury. In fact, they should begin to branch away from this problem. For example, a goal might have to do with school or work or becoming involved in a certain activity or hobby that is of interest. It may include straightening out finances, finding trusted others for support in times of distress, or planning a vacation. In any case, the goals should help the individual create new, more positive ways to define herself, build her self-esteem and self-confidence, and widen her support system. Once the patient has achieved these goals, she can create new ones. This is a never-ending process that can go on for a lifetime.

Published by FastPencil
http://www.fastpencil.com